First published 1996 by Overseas Publishers Association

Published 2016 by Routledge
2 Park Square, Milton Park, Abingdon, Oxon OX14 4RN
711 Third Avenue, New York, NY 10017, USA

Routledge is an imprint of the Taylor & Francis Group, an informabusiness.

ISBN 13: 978-3-7186-5858-9 (pbk)

Negative Page Charges
The principal author of each article will receive a voucher for his contribution in the amount of ECU 15.00 (US $20.00, Yen 3,000), which can also be used to purchase the Publisher's products directly or through university libraries, thereby reducing costs of publications to those authors supporting the journal.

This journal is sold CIF with title passing to the purchaser at the point of shipment in accordance with the laws of The Netherlands. All claims should be made to your agent or the publisher.

Distributed by International Publishers Distributor

Published in The Netherlands

MARCH 1996

Musical Performance,
1996, Vol. 1, Part 1
Reprints available directly from the publisher
Photocopying permitted by license only

Contents

Musical Performance,
1996, Vol. 1, Part 1, pp. 1–2
Reprints available directly from the publisher
Photocopying permitted by license only

Editorial

Basil Tschaikov

For a long time there has been the need for a music journal that will satisfy all music lovers – composers, performing musicians and their audiences. One that will deal with musical matters seriously and in depth in a manner that is comprehensible to those who may not be specialists in that particular field of music. *Musical Performance* is dedicated to that end. At the same time *Musical Performance* will seek to bring together the current state of knowledge in as wide an area of musical performance as possible; to stimulate further study, and to inaugurate study in areas that are changing, developing, and arising worldwide.

This first issue is *Reflections*, produced in association with the Music Performance Research Centre (MPRC) in London. The MPRC's *raison d'être* is providing the opportunity for all music lovers, composers, performers, students, researchers, and those who may only wish to hear music for its own sake, to listen (and in some cases see, as well) recordings of public performances of the always increasing past, which are otherwise not available. In this issue Jon Tolansky, its Administrator, outlines the formation and development of the Centre and the many hurdles that had to be surmounted before its inauguration. He also provides, in the final article in this issue, a selective catalogue of the current MPRC holdings of archive-recordings, audio and video, available to visitors to the Centre's Listening Studio.

The voice of the musician engaged in performing in the concert hall or opera house is rarely heard, nor do we hear from members of the audience, other than in the writings of professional critics. In this issue a conductor has the opportunity to respond to questions about opera in translation, and other questions relating to opera; a singer writes about the difficulties and rewards of taking the title role in three very different productions of a remarkable opera; two of London's distinguished orchestral musicians describe their journey into the profession and provide an insight into the joys and perils involved in that hazardous profession; an ardent concert and opera lover relates his feelings when listening to music in various environments, and describes the different levels of enjoyment of doing so, alone and in the company of others.

There are also articles about Sir Thomas Beecham and Igor Stravinsky, the development of the National Discography, soon to be within reach of all with access to the Internet.

The next issue of *Musical Performance* is concerned with the contemporary performance of Arab and Jewish traditional music in Israel. This will be followed by an issue devoted to Chinese traditional music.

The Performance of Arab and Jewish Music in Israel Today is Guest Edited by the distinguished scholar and writer on Hebrew Music Professor Amnon Shiloah. He has assembled a remarkable group of specialists who between them cover an extraordinary range of subjects: *The Judeo–Spanish Sephardi Repertoire; The Musical and Social Aspects of Belly Dancing; Ashkenazi Liturgical Music; The Performance of Arab Music in Israel; Klezmers and Their Music in Israel.*

Tradition and Change in the Performance of Chinese Music Today is Guest Edited by Dr Tsao Penyeh, Senior Lecturer in Ethnomusicology at the Chinese University in Hong Kong. Most of the contributors to this issue are resident in mainland China.

Musical Performance will not restrict the use of the phrase 'music lover' to those who enjoy 'serious' or 'classical' music. Future issues will be concerned with as wide a range of music and matters that effect musicians and audiences as possible. Topics already in hand include: the influence of rock music and recording on regional and local musics; music in broadcasting; the symphony orchestra: an instrument for the 21st century? the emotional and physical hazards of a performing career; authenticity; is it possible? jazz: past and future; performance practice and audience expectations in the 20th century.

We are particularly keen to interact with our readers. Contributions, in the form of letters, responding to material in each issue for inclusion in following issues, suggestions for topics, and articles for publication will be welcomed.

Please send all correspondence to:

The Editor
Musical Performance
Harwood Academic Publishers GmbH
PO Box 90
Reading RG1 8JL
United Kingdom

Musical Performance,
1996, Vol. 1, Part 1, pp. 3–8
Reprints available directly from the publisher
Photocopying permitted by license only

The Music Performance Research Centre: An Entry into Britain's Archive of Public Performances

Jon Tolansky

Jon Tolansky, Administrator of the Music Performance Research Centre outlines the history and purpose of this unique organisation.

Ever since the arrival of the portable cassette recorder music lovers have wished that it was possible for them to make recordings at public performances.

It has always been possible for the public to record concerts and operas that are broadcast and very many of these off-air recordings have been made, even as long ago as the 1930s, when they were taken down on acetate discs. However, though some of these are of considerable historical as well as musical value, they can only be listened to in a private, domestic situation.

In 1982, four musicians in London decided that it was worth attempting to create an Archive in which recordings made on location at public performances and those taken off-air could be housed where the public could have easy access to them.

It took another five years before the legitimate fears of the representatives of the artists (the Musicians' Union, Agents, Actor's Equity), composers and publishers, and the organizations collecting fees and royalties (the Performing Rights Society, Mechanical Copyright Protection Society) were allayed, and appropriate safeguards, encapsulated in agreements, were completed.

A major concern was the possibility of material being pirated. Both off-air recordings and some made surreptitiously on location in concert halls and opera houses had found their way into an active and profitable industry which had developed as a result of music lovers wishing to hear the reality of 'live performances': performances with the spontaneity and freshness that occurs so much more frequently at public performances than in the commercial recording studios.

At last, in 1987, with considerable assistance from the Musicians' Union, the Mechanical Copyright Protection Society, the broadcasters and many others, the Music Performance Research Centre (MPRC) was established as a company limited by guarantee with charitable status (Charity Number 296895). Since 1989 it has been possible for music lovers, performers, students, indeed anyone, to listen to a large collection of archive-recordings of public performances at the MPRC Listening Studio (Figure 1).

The MPRC Listening Studio is within the Barbican Library, at the Barbican Centre, and is open throughout the week. No charge is made for this facility. The Barbican Centre, in the City of London, is a very large arts complex containing a large concert hall, theatres, cinemas, art gallery and a library. It is the ideal venue for the MPRC Listening Studio (Figure 2).

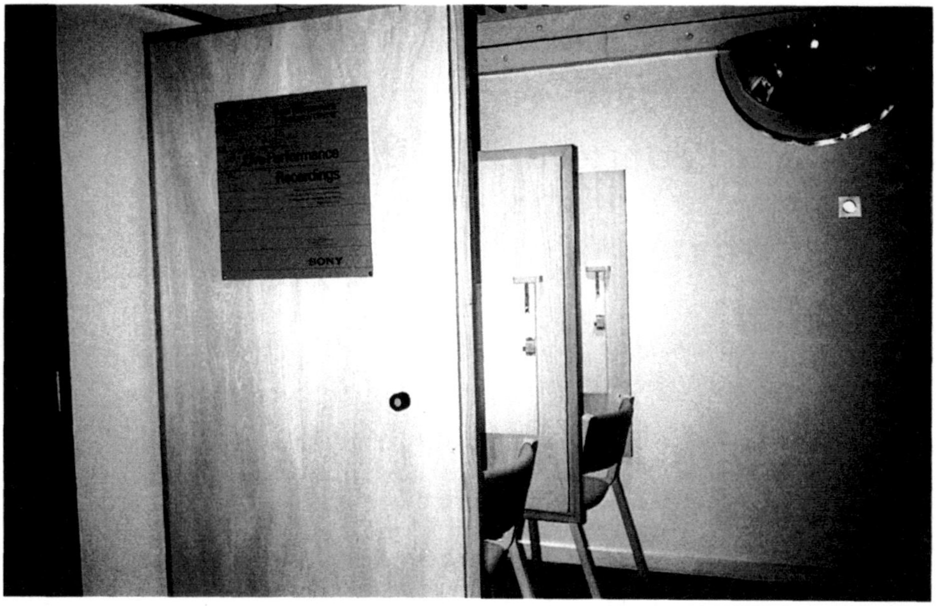

Figure 1 The MPRC Listening Studio.

Figure 2 The Barbican Centre.

Although the acquisition (legally possible for the MPRC since 1990) of valuable off-air recordings of public performances made before the establishment of the MPRC in 1987 is an important element, the primary function of the MPRC is continuing to make recordings so that in 20, 50, 100 years time, it will be possible for those who are interested to gain some impression of how music was performed before their own day. How we all wish we could hear Mozart, Beethoven and Berlioz making music; hear the legendary performers – Paganini, Liszt, Mahler; not be dependent solely on the personal recollections (and prejudices) of critics and other observers.

Now, at the MPRC, one *can* hear how Stravinsky conducted the Firebird Suite with the New Philharmonia in 1965; how Kathleen Ferrier sang Mahler's Third Symphony with Sir Adrian Boult and the BBC Symphony Orchestra in 1947; how Toscanini conducted Beethoven's Ninth Symphony with the BBC Symphony Orchestra in 1937; how Guido Cantelli and The Philharmonia performed Debussy and Schumann in front of the public in 1954; how Placido Domingo and Carlos Kleiber interpreted Verdi's "Otello" at Covent Garden in 1980; how Sir Colin Davis and the LSO performed Berlioz's The "Trojans" in 1993. At the end of this journal there is a catalogue of some of the highlights of this collection. It includes off-air recordings from the past, dating from the 1930s onwards, and on-site and off-air recordings made by the MPRC since 1987.

As far as is known, very few, if any, of the recordings at the MPRC Listening Studio can be heard elsewhere. None have been recorded commercially. There are other archives of recorded performances (mostly the property of broadcasting organizations, concert halls and opera houses), but this material is not available to the public; and there are several public archives at which some off-air broadcasts may be heard by the public. The MPRC is unique in being dedicated to the preservation of archive-recordings of public performances, on-site and off-air, and being legally empowered to accept off-air recordings that have been made in unauthorised conditions.

It will come as no surprise that security has from the start been a major preoccupation. At the listening booths at the MPRC Listening Studio (Figure 3), controls allow for increasing/decreasing volume, and advance and replay. But under no circumstances can the recordings themselves be handled, borrowed or copied.

The willing co-operation of all concerned – performing artists, composers, their agents, representatives, and those responsible for maintaining the integrity of all the rights involved – depends on the absolute security of this unique recorded material, so that exploitation of any kind is impossible.

Those involved in creating the MPRC had to overcome the natural inhibitions some artists had. It was necessary to convince the international community of artists that a different attitude to archive-recordings was required. It must be remembered that it had never been possible, or even conceivable, that any recordings could be made, other than within the confines of the commercial recording studio, or on rare occasions, on site. Of course, all recordings were financially rewarded.

The feelings and attitudes of very many performers, composers and others are highly complex, and sometimes even ambivalent. Some performers are justifiably concerned that an archive-recording may preserve a performance, or part of

Figure 3 The MPRC Listening Booths.

a performance, that they are unhappy about. And yet at the same time, they may very much wish that their ephemeral public performances should not be lost to posterity.

It was essential that the MPRC create circumstances that would overcome these fears. Only a legally binding constitution and a consent procedure that would protect all rights could provide the confidence necessary for a successful relationship between artists and the MPRC. Achieving these conditions took time and perserverance.

A Council of Management was elected under an independent chairman. The first members of the Council were representatives of the performing venues, broadcasting organisations and, by mandate, the Musicians' Union (MU) and Mechanical Copyright Protection Society (MCPS). Subsequently, a representative of the Corporation of London was elected to the Council.

Once the MPRC had been constituted, with the essential presence of the MU and MCPS, performers and composers in particular felt confident. When suitable contracts and consents had been drawn up it became possible for archive-recordings to be made on location in concert halls and opera houses.

The procedure for obtaining consents proved outstandingly successful. Most of the orchestras and solo artists contacted gave their agreement and approval for the MPRC to make archive-recordings of their performances. And so, in 1987, the MPRC became operational as the first archive specifically established to preserve public performances of music. Two years later, in 1989, it opened its Listening Studio in the Barbican Library. As at March 1995, it has recorded more than 100 performances at venues such as the Barbican Centre, Royal Festival Hall, Royal Opera House, Covent Garden, and Symphony Hall, Birmingham.

The MPRC has also been preserving many invaluable privately made recordings of performances that have been taken down off-air since the 1930s and which since 1990 it has been able to accept. These recordings would otherwise not be available to the public. They have been donated to the MPRC in accordance with a new copyright safeguard that protects performers' and composers' rights. At March 1995, more than 100 recordings have been donated, including performances by legendary artists of the past.

Unique film and video archive-recordings of performances can now be seen and heard at the MPRC Studio. Sony United Kingdom Ltd, who provided the MPRC with equipment for recording and for the listening booths at the Studio, have now provided video viewing facilities, and the BBC Libraries and Archives Division have supplied a selection of invaluable film and video recordings of performances that are not commercially available.

The MPRC has recorded conversations with international performers as part of its archival programme, and is creating an Oral History of Musicians in Britain.

Some of the MPRC's holdings are listed in the catalogue at the end of this journal. They include recordings that reveal striking differences between some artists' studio recordings and public performances.

Researching the background to these differences is one of several reasons why the MPRC initiated an ambitious research project, "Performance Practice and Audience Expectations, 1900–2000". The findings of this project (funded by the Leverhulme Trust) will be published in a future issue of *Musical Performance*. The MPRC has investigated whether there have been changes in musicians' and audiences' attitudes to performance during this century, especially taking into account the influence of recording, broadcasting, the media and travel. As part of this enquiry the MPRC is collating responses to questionnaires sent to performers and audiences.

A great deal of printed material, interviews with artists, reviews of performances, and responses to technological innovation, published since 1900, have been examined; recordings of interviews, some recorded over the years from broadcasts, some made by the MPRC, and some made privately, have been listened to; analyses have been undertaken of various aspects of performance – style, national characteristics, and the difference between commercial studio recordings and public performances of the same music, played by the same artists, within a relatively short space of time. All the extracts used in these extensive analyses will be available at the MPRC Listening Studio with the printed material.

The MPRC's archive-recordings of public performances, whether made on-site or off-air, seek to recapture, to the extent that this is possible, the reality and excitement of what occurs when artists and audience interact.

The MPRC preserves the past for today, and today for the future.

The Music Performance Research Centre (MPRC) Listening Studio is open to the public, free of charge, in the Barbican Library, Barbican Centre, London EC2Y 8DS, 9.30 am to 5.30 pm Mondays, Wednesdays, Thursdays and Fridays, 9.30 am to 7.30 pm Tuesdays, and 9.30 am to 12.30 pm Saturdays. Appointments can be booked by telephoning England 1932 860472.

Written enquiries to the Music Performance Research Centre can be sent to The Administrator, The Music Performance Research Centre, The Barbican Library, The Barbican Centre, Silk Street, London EC2Y 8DS, or faxed to The Administrator on fax number England 1932 860472.

Musical Performance,
1996, Vol. 1, Part 1, pp. 9–19
Reprints available directly from the publisher
Photocopying permitted by license only

The Conductor Speaks: An Interview with Mark Elder

Mark Elder

Mark Elder was Music Director of the English National Opera between 1979 and 1993, during which time he initiated radical changes in its artistic policies and standards that brought it international recognition. From 1989 to 1994 he was Music Director of the Rochester Philharmonic Orchestra, USA, and from 1992 to 1995 Principal Guest Conductor of the City of Birmingham Symphony Orchestra.

The Music Performance Research Centre asked Mark Elder for his views on several issues, including the future of opera, translations of libretti, attitudes to productions, and the role of the conductor past and present.

Do you think the Music Director should be in control of all the elements of an opera production?

No, I don't believe this is possible. The best results happen in collaboration. If you invite someone to do a production, you discuss the work and the casting with them. In the process of casting you find out something about that person's attitude towards the opera. In my experience, for instance, the age of a singer is very often of the smallest significance in the achievement of a performance. But when a director is casting he often puts incredible importance on it. For instance, the King in "Lohengrin", King Henry the Fowler, is a figure of great authority, gravitas, wisdom and maturity. The singer who sang the role recently at ENO is in his middle twenties. He has talent and potential that I hope he will develop – but as the figure of the King he already seemed to me to be very good. He's a big guy, but he's very young (Figure 1). Similarly, when an artist is much older than the part to be played. If a singer can sing the part and can imbue their imagination with the requisite approach, their age is often not the most important factor.

In the preparation of an opera the director's job is to prepare the visual world and he does that with some reference to the conductor. The director has to involve himself in the piece and respond to it as best he may – as I do with the score – sometimes years in advance. Some of the pieces that I have conducted in the last 10 years I've lived with for more than 20 years. I like to see a model of the set, and hear how his ideas are going. And there have been times when I have said 'How are we going to cope with this moment in the middle act when such and such has to happen?'; perhaps he's forgotten about it, or hasn't really thought it through, and he needs to take that on board. Designers and producers are thinking of the visual world and not necessarily about solving all the problems that the score poses. The German director Joachim Herz first came to do "Salomé" with us at ENO in the 1970s, then "Fidelio", and then I did "Madam Butterfly" with him in

Figure 1 Linda McLeod as Elsa and Michael Druiett as Henry the Fowler in a scene from English National Opera's production of Wagner's 'Lohengrin' at the London Coliseum in October 1993; produced by Tim Albery and conducted by Mark Elder. Photographer: Richard Mildenhall. By permission of English National Opera.

Berlin. He was a consummate musician, and he was very courageous as well as very demanding, of himself and me. We had difficult moments, but on the whole it was a good collaboration because I knew that he understood what I was doing, respected it and listened to me. That is quite rare. Not every director is free enough or confident enough musically to really listen to what the conductor is trying to achieve. When it happens, it is very exciting, because it inspires one to do better. During my time with ENO I would say that there were an equal number of productions when the staging balanced the music and when it overbalanced it. I think that as the1980s progressed the pressure increased for designers and directors to compete with the incredible financial backing that musicals received. In addition, the immense popularity of cinema meant that the pressure of competition on our opera house was enormous. The Coliseum has the widest stage in England; it has a very large area for a designer to fill and, of course, there are many ways of doing this. You can do it with massive emptiness or enormous constructive ingenuity. And we have seen examples of both. There is a need to appeal to all audiences – potential cinema-goers, and those who enjoy musicals, as well as keen opera-lovers.

In particular, people who had never been to an opera house had to be persuaded to find their way into the Coliseum under the right circumstances and be introduced to what we had to offer. This happened more and more throughout the 1980s. It didn't happen every night, but I believed it was essential for the company's future to be doing much, much more than we were in the 1970s to break down elitism, break down the barriers, making sure that, as far as we could, ticket prices were pitched at a level which wouldn't be too prohibitive to the majority of people. I think we did encourage a more informal attitude on the part of the audience. People come now dressed as they would like to be, not feeling that they have to dress up. The theatre should be a centre of the community's life – be a cultural meeting point – a place where ideas can be shared and expressed, where the hottest disagreements as well as the strongest unity of opinion can be expressed. Our worst enemy is indifference; we need to be able to agree to disagree. I shall never forget the first time the audience erupted into a frenzy of both booing and cheering in the middle of an opera!

Traditionally the theatre has always been a meeting place of attitudes and opinions, and I felt that as we came out of the 1970s there weren't enough evenings that really stimulated the audience. As Brecht used to say "the audience must not hang up its head with its hat". In the end, if we developed a "house style", it was in the diversity of approaches to be found in our work.

Sometimes there were occasions when as music director I had to lay down the law over design ideas. In the end these things have to be thrashed out and a compromise has to be reached. There can be certain instances when a director is pushing for a particular visual solution that doesn't appeal to me. The evolution of a production on the other hand, comes in rehearsals. If you're going to try and achieve a totally integrated performance it cannot be put together in two weeks; it takes five or six. Four weeks in the rehearsal studio and two weeks in the theatre, at least, are required to achieve an integrated performance. Of course, it is possible to do with less, but you won't find the singers particularly relating to one another, or functioning together as a group of human beings on the stage. Their eyes will more likely be glued to the conductor in order to keep the music together! Many performances in Europe take place night after night without any rehearsal at all. Everyone's expertise and experience is absolutely crucial. But if you're trying to build up a cast that's prepared to be an ensemble, where the conductor knows when he must accommodate the singers and breathe with the production, and when he must insist that they are in contact with him, so that the musical standards are maintained – that is something that needs time. The analogy for me is: you will never make a good chilli in one cooking! It must be allowed to sit on the back burner; you add a little bit more and then a bit more, and gradually you get that fullness of flavour.

Do you feel it is a serious problem for you that many opera companies lack sufficient serious rehearsal time?

It depends on the quality of the ingredients! Even with little or no rehearsal, a performance can be immensely exciting when everyone is on form. I recently made my debut in the Bavarian State Opera performances of Verdi's "La Forza del Destino" and Richard Strauss's "Salomé". Both without rehearsal. No rehearsal at all!

I think it's fun under those circumstances to have a couple of rehearsals – to leave some things without rehearsal – leave them till the performance, but be able to try and draw some unity into the performance. A good opera conductor has to have spent years in the theatre. But unfortunately this is rather unfashionable nowadays.

How important do you think it is for a young conductor to gain experience in the opera house?

I was lucky to be given opportunities early on in my career that helped me learn my craft technically and artistically in the theatre. For me it became a passion, and the joining together of all the musical and theatrical interests I had as a teenager. I had acted quite a lot both at school and university; I sang as a child, and I played different instruments; opera brought all this together. The problem for conductors coming into the opera house who have not had this experience is that they don't know how the music will work in the theatre as opposed to working in their mind. The Italian conductor Carlo Maria Giulini said once "we conduct opera for two things: to learn how music can express psychology of character, and how all music must breathe". Singers cannot begin a phrase unless they have had the space to take their breath so as to allow the phrase to happen. And wind players in orchestras also need that space. Working with singers helps us to realize that all music has to have that eternal sense of giving and taking. Sometimes you have to urge on the singer, other times encourage them to take more time.

What were some of your visions for ENO?

At the English National Opera I wanted to develop a regular audience that would be prepared to experiment with us – take us on trust. In that sense I saw the company needing to be entrenched in the community. Of course, in the middle of a capital city the size of London, "the community" was difficult to define, but I knew that people regularly came to see our productions from many miles away. The absence of any touring as part of our annual programme was in my view greatly to be regretted – it was simply a financial impossibility. The Arts Council were in no position, year after year, to make up any loss that we might incur on a tour. And as our repertoire became more and more built especially for the size of the Coliseum, any touring would need an enormous expenditure to adapt the productions to smaller theatres. So it was impossible for us to take on four weeks touring without incurring a substantial deficit, which the Arts Council could not make up.

During the 13 or 14 years I was Music Director the orchestra changed considerably, both in sound quality and personnel. Developing the sound of an orchestra cannot be done overnight. It comes as the result of trust and the desire within the orchestra to improve. I think it is true to say that my relationship with the orchestra was very difficult in the first five years. I felt that certain changes in personnel and work practices were long overdue. That is very difficult for an orchestra to accept. It is very important to listen to the orchestra's point of view, but inevitably there were disagreements.

However, the point is that the orchestra did, little by little, change its attitude. Many of the changes of personnel were not, of course, instigated by me. Players go to other orchestras, take other positions, want a change of life, or retire. And I think you would be surprised at the number of players in the orchestra who really love opera. A good opera orchestra listens to the singers and goes with them and respects them. They will always respond to beautiful singing. I have noticed this time and time again in all sorts of different repertoire; if a singer is on particularly good form the orchestra will always notice! That's very thrilling! Another aspect of our relationship is that the orchestra has seen me develop as well. It has been a two-way partnership.

I demanded more of the orchestra, but I said that in return I would try and find conductors who would get the best out of them. But I also had to do something about the basic salary rates. At the beginning of the 1980s we did start to change the way the orchestra was paid. A significant breakthrough came when the Inland Revenue decided that the orchestra could all be taxed in the same way. Until then some members of the orchestra had been obliged to pay a good deal more tax than others and this had been the cause of a lot of bitterness.

Would you like to have conducted ballet – should there have been ballet at the English National Opera, as there is at The Royal Opera House, Covent Garden?

Conducting ballet is as much its own craft as conducting opera. Good conductors of ballet have to understand the way a dancer breathes and moves – when they need time and when they don't. This is a separate skill and it requires just as many years of passion, dedication and training as learning to conduct opera well. It's a pity that there aren't more first-class conductors of ballet, because some of the greatest scores have been written for the great ballet companies and still continue to be written; it's a very exciting medium. I find myself drawn more to modern dance than classical ballet. To have a musical performance of a ballet you need a very special relationship between the conductor, choreographer, and dancers. And it would need amazing patience on the part of the conductor to work out the choreography with the choreographer so that the conductor's tempi are respected and that the conductor feels confident enough in his tempi to say no, no, it can't go that slow!!

But I think it is idealistic to think of having one conductor for both opera and ballet, a ballet company deserves to have its own music director, and to be music director of a ballet company as well as an opera company would be asking too much.

A major question for everyone concerned with opera is whether it should always be performed in the original language or in the vernacular. What is your opinion?

A huge issue! One I have been involved in for 25 years. It's a question of to what extent you are interested in understanding what an opera is about. In very large cities like New York, Paris or London, it's to the public's benefit to have two opera houses that perform complementary tasks, provided it's done to the highest possible standard in both. I believe that when circumstances are at its best, it is possible for an audience that does not know the libretto and does not speak the original language, to derive much more fascination and enrichment from being able to understand most of the words of an opera as they are sung. I've conducted performances and often sat in the audience when that has been the case. When we did a new production of "The Marriage of Figaro", we commissioned a new translation. It was a very well-designed set, an expert cast, brilliantly rehearsed. The title of the opera had been changed, almost as a warning to the audience, to "Figaro's Wedding". People now refer to it as Figaro's Wedding, which is great. The pleasure of being in an audience and hearing this wonderful libretto, interestingly, carefully translated, and being articulated with maximum comprehension was a thrilling experience. Two thousand people were hearing this great comedy of sex manners. It was being laughed at, and sympathised with as the words came out of the mouths of the singers. I think the comprehension in "Lohengrin", on the other hand, was not quite as good as I would have liked it to have been. I don't think it was Wagner's fault. I think it's really a question of the problems of singing these roles and articulating the text in a large theatre. But there is no reason why performances of "Rigoletto" or "La Traviata" shouldn't be totally intelligible to the public.

Of course, a translation is, by definition, a compromise. I have never known a composer or read about a composer who didn't want his pieces to be understood by the audience. But the problems of translation are huge. The best ones are often those that have been worked on by a group. There is nothing sacrosanct, in my view, about a translated text. Tastes change; singers have different strengths; the input of the director and conductor is important to the final result. Music imposes so many strictures on the translation – you have to be a terrier! Honing and scratching away to find better solutions.

Working with David Pountney was particularly enjoyable. David is a first-class musician and a very experienced translator. When he and I have done translations together he has sent me scenes as he has done them. I make comments, and he comes up with improvements. When we did "La Traviata", "Hansel and Gretel" and "Königskinder" everything was done well before rehearsals began and the number of changes that were made later were very few and far between. Generally, it's a much more arduous process. I believe that the contribution that the musician must make must be to decide, note by note, whether the music can be changed or not. I myself hold the view that to aim to make a translation that does not change the music *at all* is a completely false aim. One can see this by comparing what Strauss started to do when he tried to put "Salomé" back into Oscar Wilde's original French. There are printed scores available for comparison. Now, when we think of the opening of "Salomé", famous for having no overture, the first line of the text is there within the first few bars of the score. The German text is "Wie schön ist die Prinzessin Salomé heute Nacht!" The French text has exactly the same meaning, but of course the words have different lengths and accents. Strauss changed the music completely to fit the natural accentuation of the French text. In another context, Verdi said "when you change Macbeth into French, make sure you don't change the place of the word 'follie' ", ('madness, madness', the French word 'folie' is exactly the same). He wanted to make sure that it came in exactly the same place in the music because he believed that the effect of that particular word was incredibly important for the impact of the whole number. He

Figure 2 The Tower Scene from Debussy's 'Pelléas et Melisande', in the English National Opera production by David Pountney at the London Coliseum in 1990, with Cathryn Pope as Melisande and Thomas Randle as Pelléas, conducted by Mark Elder. Photographer: Anthony Crickmay. By permission of English National Opera.

was absolutely right. But it's very difficult to put that word into English or find something that matches it. In my experience translators aren't necessarily the best judges of where the music should be altered. This may surprise a lot of people but, in the heat of the moment, nobody in the audience asks themselves what has been changed in that bar, in that phrase? If the result is convincing, then it is right.

"Pelléas et Melisande" is a good example. A Maeterlinck play that was set without changing the original: cuts were made, but very few lines were altered in changing it into an operatic text. It gave Debussy exactly what he was hoping for, because the shadows in the play, the feelings underneath the lines, were exactly what he needed for his own musical inspiration. The way the text is set has all the fluidity he wanted. It lacks the strong accents and definite pulse beats that characterise Anglo-Saxon languages. So you could say that to do "Pelléas" in any other language than French is a waste of time. It would so falsify the original that you would lose much, much more than you would gain. Indeed, Sadlers Wells Opera in the 1960s, prepared a new production of "Pelléas and Melisande" when I think Colin Davis, the Music Director, was going to conduct it. They organised the translation, they printed up the vocal scores and then cancelled it because the management didn't believe in the exercise. I have seen that translation and I wouldn't believe in it either. In my view far too great a respect had been paid to the original vocal lines. I've done "Pelléas" now in two productions in London (Figure 2), both of course in English, both fundamentally the same translation. I chose this particular translator because he believed, as I did, that what was more important was the literal translation of this very direct text, and the consequent adjustment of the vocal lines.

We had to prepare a completely new vocal score with the original voice parts set out and with enough space to put another whole vocal stave in to make the rhythmic alterations clear. There's scarcely a bar unaltered. To take one example; Melisande's first line is famously: 'Ne me touchez pas, ne me touchez pas . . .' 'Don't touch me, don't touch me, or I'll throw myself in the water.' And the music has to be altered to make the English seem natural. Anything else sounds like a translation – it sounds like a compromise. The proof of the pudding is in the eating. The ear always has to be the guide. When I did the second production of "Pelléas", two or three years ago, there were things I had changed before that I now felt were to the detriment of the music. I altered a few notes in "Lohengrin" as well, so that the important syllable fell on a better note. This will usually be when a declamatory phrase is involved – very rarely indeed in a lyrical phrase. So there is a very creative element in all this. And it can take months and months! The problem for the singers is where does it finish? When the words sound as if they could have been what the composer originally set, I answer!

Now that surtitles have become much more common the question arises as to whether any translation is required.

There are really two issues here. What should an audience be offered? And how does it involves me as a conductor and as an interested operatic musician? I think that if an audience is drawn into an opera by surtitles and they get more out of the experience, it has to be a good thing for the future of opera. Whether or not surtitles are here to stay, I suspect the advantages more than outweigh the disadvantages. The greatest disadvantage is that it keeps the whole thing relentlessly at one remove. People are actually looking at surtitles and responding to the surtitles and not to the performance itself. The angle of vision is a practical problem, which in films, and television, completely disappears. But there is no substitute for the visual thrill of excitement – of understanding – then and there – of seeing the interchange, and hearing the conversation – and consequently sharing the feeling.

Do you feel that as a musician you should communicate with your audience using film, broadcasting, and so on, rather as Leonard Bernstein did?

Yes, I do. I recently made a film about Verdi.[1] I wrote, devised, and presented it on camera and on the rostrum. It's the first time I've ever been involved in a documentary film of this nature. It's something that I spent five years dreaming about, and the sixth year doing. It was a very large project. It was directed by Barrie Gavin who has spent 30 years making films about music for British and German television.

I have tried to portray the weight, range and temperament of this incredible character who had such a long life throughout the 19th century. To try and marry up the enormous understanding, vigour and humanity of his operas with his rather rugged, intractable, personality. The slant of the film is to try and show how he spent so much time, in the second half of his life, back in the countryside near Parma where he was born. It was an attempt to find some peace and proportion in his life which had been spent travelling so many thousands of miles to all the different cities of the world to honour commissions that he had agreed to do.

Do you feel that film and TV will be good for opera?

I think that film, generally, has enormous potential for the future of live music. Having such vast audiences it can bring people to understand and appreciate a whole range of things with which they would otherwise not have any contact. With Verdi, for instance, perhaps the best way to think about him as a whole person is to listen to the music; the way it develops and changes in his extraordinary long career. The film contrasts the incredible power and passion of his operas with the restraint of his personal life and the difficulties he had in organizing it. The film has over one hour of specially recorded music. Orchestral extracts from his operas provide us with contrast and background music during the film. A number of carefully selected scenes from his operas were specially rehearsed and filmed with some very fine singers, English National Opera chorus, and the orchestra of English National Opera. All the scenes are sung in Italian, and in one instance French. Because it's for television, the texts can be subtitled.

[1] *Verdi – a life in two parts*. Dir. Barrie Gavin. BBC.

When it goes to other non-English speaking countries, either my voice will be dubbed over, or there will be sub-titles.

I believe that musicians more and more need to learn how to communicate with a broader audience. I've tried to do this sometimes from the podium, on television, and on radio, particularly in America where there is a great hunger for it. The conductor can lead his audience into the experience of listening to the music. Bernstein developed his own incredible talents. It's something I'm trying to do as well. It's fascinating just trying to find the right tone. After all, the last thing you need to enjoy a concert is a university degree! You have to open your ears and your heart and be happy to take the music as you find it and not be worried or self-conscious about your reactions.

I want to make every effort to get as close to my audience as possible. We should all communicate our enthusiasm and passion and what we feel about the music. After its courtly beginnings, opera was designed to appeal to the widest possible range of people. At the première of an opera in Italy, the baker could be expected to be there alongside the teacher or the judge. There should be no feeling that music is only for people of a certain social status. The greatness of Verdi is that he wrote music to appeal to every level of society.

Film can be such a good way of communicating with the widest possible audience. Of course it is another craft, a whole new discipline for me. Knowing how to say things as coherently as possible within the limited time that is at your disposal. Finding the right tone of voice so that people feel that they are being brought into something, that you're sharing an enthusiasm with them. This is something that I believe is very important for the future of music. I hope that there will be other topics that could be equally as arresting. There are other favourite composers of mine that I think would lend themselves wonderfully to a filmic treatment.

Do you perform in just the same way whether you are working in the recording studio, concert hall, or opera house?

I think the art of making good recordings in the studio, if they're done without prior rehearsal and performance, is a rather different art from preparing a performance for public consumption – immediately, a one-off live performance. It's a question of skilful use of resources and time in the studio. Knowing how to make the best use of a particular studio: knowing how to get the best results from long takes or short patching takes. All this is part of the craft of a conductor more than his skill as an interpreter.

My view is that the more sophisticated recording equipment becomes, and the more 'perfect' the results can be, the greater the need will be for live performance, the thrill of actually seeing and hearing artists make it happen at that moment. The musical theatre, of course, stands at the forefront of this need for the visual excitement of live performance. I believe that this is one of the reasons why opera seems to continue to attract people. More and more small and larger opera companies are being formed – let's hope that the money is found from somewhere to support them! To sit in a full opera house as part of an audience that is responding to a great opera is unforgettable. A recording equivalent can never replace that.

Have you been influenced by recordings made by some of the great conductors of the past?

Listening to recordings of some of the greatest conductors gives me ideas, challenges me. It may not be my way, but it has its own integrity. In the last ninety years, there have been many fine conductors. In today's world, the concept of 'greatness' all too often seems to be exaggerated by commercial considerations. Ultimately, a *really* great performance lingers in the mind. What marks out the genuinely lasting over the good and solid is the conductor's ability to inspire his players and, with them, to communicate the music vividly to the audience.

Musical Performance,
1996, Vol. 1, Part 1, pp. 21–29
Reprints available directly from the publisher
Photocopying permitted by license only

The Death of Boris: Performing the Role of Moussorgsky's Boris Godunov – Thoughts and Experiences

Robert Lloyd

Bass-baritone Robert Lloyd has been singing in the world's major opera houses for over twenty-five years. His large repertoire includes the roles King Mark in Wagner's "Tristan und Isolde", Gurnemanz in Wagner's "Parsifal", Arkel in Debussy's "Pelléas et Melisande", and Boris in Moussorgsky's "Boris Godunov". He is one of today's most sought after interpreters of the role of Boris, which he has sung in three very different productions: Andrei Tarkovsky's at the Royal Opera House Covent Garden, Harry Kupfer's at the Netherlands Opera, and Piero Faggioni's at the Florence Opera. In this article he discusses the background to the opera's creation, the strong influence of Feodor Chaliapin and Boris Christoff, two famous interpreters of the main role, and how the experience of taking on three directors' vastly different approaches to the role has affected his relationship to the part.

Of all the roles available to a bass singer one stands out far above all the rest. "Boris Godunov" is not a very long role: there are many others which are much longer – Mephistopheles, Gurnemanz, Procida, Leporello, Figaro, Rocco to name but a few – all of which are in many ways more demanding in terms of voice and musicianship. But Boris has characteristics which make it uniquely demanding and uniquely satisfying.

It is, of course, one of the very few title roles that a bass gets to sing. He can find this unwonted flush of fame and significance very exciting. As Frederick the Great said after his invasion of Silesia, "It is very beguiling to read about yourself in the newspapers". Those who play Boris can easily feel more important than they really are when momentarily in the limelight which higher voices can take for granted. There is a temptation to milk the opportunity for all it is worth and exploit the role as a star vehicle. Both Chaliapin, the great Russian bass-baritone who first brought the role of Boris to the West, and his successor Boris Christoff, the Bulgarian who monopolised the role for over twenty-five years at Covent Garden, brought a triumphalist reading to the role and applied to it all their extravagant histrionic skills, so that it has become firmly lodged in the public mind as a vehicle for a great star. This has possibly done the opera a disservice. The satisfactions of Boris run deeper than that.

Moussorgsky has provided us with an operatic masterwork of deep intelligence matched only by his own "Khovanschina". What he has contrived is a level of dramatic truth without precedent in nineteenth-century opera. When the opera is treated as a star vehicle its integrity is obscured. This dramatic truth is both emotional, as expressed in the private utterances of the man Boris, and historical, as expressed in the reaction of the Russian body politic to the phenomenon of Boris Godunov.

In both his operas Moussorgsky achieves a remarkable musical expression of a view of history. It is the view that the philosopher Karl Popper called 'historicism' – the belief that history moves in patterns. In both his operas Moussorgsky expresses a view of Russia as a great organism with its own rhythms and timetable which you disturb at your peril. In "Khovanschina" we hear in the music of the Old Believers, the folk voice of Russia, immutable, superstitious, deeply passionate, relentlessly immovable. In the music of the modernising forces of Peter the Great we hear a brassiness challenging the old order. Change is coming, but to accommodate it the old order cannot be adapted, only destroyed. The final mass self-immolation by the Old Believers is symbolic of the deeply suicidal tendencies of Russian society. Writing at the end of the nineteenth century Moussorgsky seems to have been able almost to sense the brassy sounds of Marxism in the distance, and anticipate Russia's appalling twentieth-century suicide.

Boris Godunov contains many similarly compelling historical themes. It is the story of how Russia is left in potential chaos by the demise of the House of Rurik after the death of Feodor, son of Ivan the Terrible. Boris Godunov, a commoner related only by marriage to the royal family, is elected Tsar to restore order. Because he has no legitimate claim to the throne, the body politic of Russia rejects him, like a heart transplant, and plunges back into anarchy. For me the story is about Legitimacy and the Divine Right of Kings, a concept which obsessed medieval rulers and which is still a force to be reckoned with. Even today, with the end of Communist rule in Russia, the exiled Romanovs are twitching excitedly. Without overt legitimacy a ruler must have an extraordinary amount of luck or absolute power. Boris had neither legitimacy nor luck; nor a talent or taste for tyranny.

As an elected monarch Boris's claim was never secure. Democracy had no hold on the Russian mind. Deep in their superstitious souls neither Boris, nor anyone else, believed that election was sufficient title to the throne of Russia. For some time his luck held and things went well, but when events turned against him rumours about him began to circulate. His Achilles heel was the rumour that he was implicated in the death of the child Dmitri who should have come to the throne after the death of Feodor. Modern historians tend to deny his involvement, but at the time Moussorgsky was writing it was normal to suppose Boris was guilty.

It was his Watergate. If one recalls the weeping, haunted shame of Richard Nixon one gets a whiff of Boris. In fact Nixon makes an interesting parallel study. He was for years the power behind the throne of Eisenhower and the Republican party, both as Vice-President and as Presidential candidate.

Boris was in a similar position in the reign of Ivan the Terrible. Nixon feared and hated the Ivy League aristocracy and especially the Kennedys, just as Boris feared the Boyar aristocracy and especially Prince Shuisky. Nixon's crime was attempting to secure, by illegal means, advantage in the electoral process. Boris's was manipulating the succession. In the Pushkin/Moussorgsky version Prince Shuisky plays upon Boris's guilt and hounds him to an early grave, rather as Washington hounded Nixon to a premature political death.

The Boris that Moussorgsky paints in music is surprisingly real. He has great stature. He expresses noble intentions, the frustrations of one balked in ambitious good works. He is a consummate politician, and he is a warm and considerate family man. Moussorgsky paints a character not far from historical truth. Boris was potentially a great ruler. His reign was to the grossness of Ivan the Terrible's rather as Gorbachov's was to Stalin's. Indeed he was defeated by the very same old problems that defeated Gorbachov nearly four hundred years later – Baltic insurrection, religious unrest (conflict within the Communist party), famine (shortages), pestilence (Chernobyl), lack of legitimacy (no popular mandate), and a persistent rival with a strong claim (Yeltsin). The opera "Boris Godunov" touches on many profound and startlingly contemporary political issues and opens up many stimulating lines of thought. To do justice to it, the role of Boris has to be played in a way which reveals an understanding of these issues.

When writing about the opera, the great Russian theatre philosopher Stanislavsky said that the title role demanded of a player a "very big temperament". That has certainly been my experience. No role is so demanding. There is an enormous range of emotion to express in a comparatively short time – triumph at the Coronation mixed with fear and awe at the size of the task; domestic warmth in the Nursery scene; a wide-ranging assessment of the Russian political scene in the Monologue; the exercise of power and decision-making when dealing with the Polish insurrection and with Prince Shuisky; and the rapid decline into delusion and paranoia on learning the identity the Pretender is assuming. This is followed, in the scene when he confronts the crowd in front of St. Basil's Cathedral, by the helpless despair of a man rendered impotent by events and locked up in his own sense of guilt. Finally, the death scene demands the full range of personality, switching in and out of sanity, coping with crippling physical illness, and appalled concern for the vulnerable child who will succeed him on the Throne. Then the death itself is deeply frustrated and reluctant: there is tension to the very end. He is not ready to go. Moussorgsky has written no beautiful tunes for the singer to hide behind. It is the text that determines the melodic line in a way that is unique to Moussorgsky. You have an astonishing sensation of spontaneous utterance every time you sing it. Boris is a role so brilliantly written and so exhaustingly intense to perform that, after it, almost all other operatic roles feel shallow and contrived.

It is very easy for a player to be lured into histrionic tricks, to underline or pick telling moments. I suspect Chaliapin did succumb to this temptation. The makeup he used for Boris, of which he was very proud, was truly splendid. Clearly it was designed to make Boris look as imperious and magnificent as possible – tall, black-bearded and in rich bejewelled costume. I can find nothing in the text to support this image. Moreover the real-life portrait of Boris is of a smallish, mild-faced man. Chaliapin said that when he was first preparing the role he spent many hours perfecting the 'walk'. I find that really intriguing. How does a Tsar walk? If Tsars have special walks, is there another special walk for a Tsar who is not a Tsar by right? In truth, wearing a heavy robe and holding an orb and spectre, there's only one way to walk. I can only suppose that Chaliapin was looking for a special effect quite extraneous to the text to enhance the eye-catching magnificence of the figure he cut on the stage – rather as when he sang Mephistopheles he did it half-naked in a loin cloth. Perhaps I'm maligning him. I wish there was some film footage so we could see what he really did.

I can speak from my own memory of how Boris Christoff exploited the potential of the role. His most spectacular trick was to pitch forward from a very high throne just before Boris's death. Falling from such a height made the audience

Figure 1 Robert Lloyd as Boris Godunov in Andrei Tarkovsky's production at the Royal Opera House Covent Garden in 1983, conducted by Claudio Abbado. Photograph by Christina Burton. By permission of Lies Askonas Ltd.

gasp. He was caught by six strategically placed choristers who were specially selected by Christoff for the job, and suitably rewarded at the end of the run. It was a sure fire winner as a *coup de théâtre*. It is a trick also used by many other basses but it owes its origin to Chaliapin. To my mind, marvellous though it was in its own way, it is external to the intention of the piece. Moussorgsky's "Boris Godunov" is a big enough piece not to need artificial enrichment.

Certainly when I came to play the role I had to fight my way through a maze of preconceived ideas and established tradition, both in myself and in those around me. I was deluged with advice, most of it, although well meant, bearing the dead hand of convention. I am sure I would not have been strong enough to fight my way through these without the extreme good fortune of working with three really outstanding opera producers. It might be interesting to compare their different approaches.

The first production was at the Royal Opera House Covent Garden (Figure 1). The great Russian film director Andrei Tarkovsky was turning to opera for the first time when he produced Boris at the ROH. He brought with him the extraordinary sensitivity and intellectual honesty and openness which are so much the hallmark of his films. He certainly had no time for the traditions of the opera. "We will not pretend that anything is something it is not", he said at the start of rehearsals. "We will not pretend that you are Boris Godunov. You will always be Robert Lloyd. We will not pretend that the scenery is real. We will know that it is wood and polystyrene. We will not pretend that the orchestra is not there; it will be at every performance". I found this a tough concept to come to grips with. The effect of grappling with it as an idea was to throw me onto my inner resources and onto the score that Moussorgsky had provided as our raw material.

What the Tarkovsky production showed was the distinction between dramatic truth, which he sought, and dramatic realism, which he was not bothered with. There was no attempt to show the settings of the events portrayed. The designs were by the distinguished Franco-Russian painter Nicholas Dvigubsky. They suggested a society in disarray, in transition and insecure of its foundations. The set was fundamentally a ramp on which all the main action took place. This was surrounded by a redbrick wall with ramparts still under construction. The stage on each side of the ramp was bare except for being littered with broken artefacts and weapons – the debris of the past. Perhaps we were intended to perceive Boris's Russia as a society trying to escape from the rubbish of its past and constructing a new social edifice for the future. The set was practical for operatic purposes, providing plenty of movement space for the chorus, but unspecific enough to keep the minds of the audience open to the issues raised in the drama.

We had to work almost entirely without furniture or props, which was a great challenge. Stanislavsky would have been proud of us for the way we drew structure from the text and from inside ourselves rather than relying on externals. The force of Tarkovsky's concept of 'not pretending' became clear in the Nursery scene. Here the only furniture was a huge tapestry which was part drape and part carpet. (Figure 2). It was a map of Russia. It proved to be all we needed to develop a spontaneous and unpremeditated *coup de théâtre*, which for me will always be one of the highlights of my life. The carpet became the centre of the scene. By turns it became a homely space for sitting on with one's children, a classroom for instructing the young Tsarevich the geography of Russia, a private zone from which all strangers were excluded, and thus a focus for the growing paranoia of

Figure 2 Robert Lloyd as Boris Godunov on producer Andrei Tarkovsky's carpet, at the Royal Opera House Covent Garden in 1983. Photograph by Christina Burton. By permission of Lies Askonas Ltd.

Boris, and finally a duvet or comforter for him to wrap himself in as he disintegrates into madness and childish vulnerability.

The other notably unconventional element in this production was the death scene. This death was a humiliating affair. The stricken Boris pitched full length on the floor and crawled painfully towards his throne with the idea of occupying it on behalf of his son. In fact he only succeeded in upsetting it on top of his son and then expired clutching at the air like a man drowning in quicksands. It was a compelling image, but I was inundated with advice from all quarters by those who remembered Christoff's triumphalist death. I was 'missing my opportunity'. One newspaper called it risible. To me and to Tarkovsky it seemed the perfect expression of the tragedy of Boris. It is the essence of tragedy that it should be tragic. This was a personal tragedy for Boris, but also a public tragedy for Russia. He had left his country a legacy of anarchy. In the transition to the final scene Boris's corpse was scooped up like a bag of rubbish and unceremoniously thrown away.

Tarkovsky wanted one final flourish which rather fortunately he had to abandon because of the limitations of the Covent Garden stage. He wanted the soul of Boris to rise from his corpse and be lifted to heaven by angels. This idea which seemed uncharacteristically kitschy caused us all a great deal of anxiety, but was clearly very important to Tarkovsky. I came to realise that he saw this production of *Boris* as an opportunity to make a very personal testament. This included a statement of his own Christianity. Unfortunately for him in the West expressions of religious belief do not have the same resonances as they did in what was then a Marxist Russia whose regime Tarkovsky had come to loathe. I think it was this personalising of the production that gave it an edge of sensitivity beyond all the other productions I have done. And it was a sensitivity which was lost almost immediately. Tarkovsky died only a matter of months after this production and without him we were never able to rediscover that same delicacy of touch in subsequent revivals.[1]

If sensitivity was the watchword of Tarkovsky's production, the one by Harry Kupfer, at Het Musikteater in Amsterdam, was the exact reverse. This production had its origins in Kupfer's own Komische Oper in what was then Communist East Berlin within sight of the infamous Wall, that symbol of totalitarian repression. Kupfer, too, used the opera to make a personal statement. Clearly his aim was to express his hatred of totalitarian Russia. He apologised for speaking no Russian. 'I only studied it for seven years at school', he said with heavy irony.

Kupfer productions are notorious for their brutal personal relations. This was no exception. The set was a series of cages into which the chorus (i.e. the Russian people) were herded by armed guards with whips. There was no suggestion of glamour. Even the Coronation robe was made of steel reflective plates creating a gaudy and tasteless expression of power. There was no suggestion of a specific location. This was not geographical Russia, only the bleak angular soullessness of a notional totalitarianism. Boris however was not included in this. His costume was a white satin cassock and the impression he gave was of a saintly influence propelled, *force majeur*, into a kind of hysterical brutality and constant panic.

One particular made this production markedly different from others. Boris's son Feodor is normally played by a young mezzo-soprano, as Moussorgsky intended. In this production he was played by the German counter-tenor Jochan Kowalski, who was young enough to pass on stage as a sixteen year old. This is rather older than the real Feodor, but Kupfer felt this was a sacrifice of a small reality in pursuit of a greater truth. It meant that it was impossible to play the death scene sentimentally. It is very easy to clutch a young woman to your bosom, stroke her hair feelingly and reliably jerk a tear. It is more difficult to do it if the Feodor is a man almost your own size. It is more difficult because it is more real. In fact you have to find some completely different way of playing the scene. Kupfer had Boris sing all his advice to his son while at the same time pushing the reluctant young man onto the throne. As he grew weaker he slid pitifully to the floor at the boy's feet while Feodor cringed in terror at his father's desperation and at the approach of his own awful responsibilities. The device of using Kowalski certainly had the effect of preventing any phoneyness from softening the starkness of this intense drama.

It was rendered the more stark by being performed in Moussorgsky's original version, that is without an interval, and lasting just over two hours, because it did not include the Polish scenes. These scenes were written later by Moussorgsky to

[1] Andrei Tarkovsky's production of "Boris Godunov" was staged in 1983 at the Royal Opera House, Covent Garden, with Claudio Abbado conducting.

accommodate the demand for a female character, some love interest and some courtly glamour – all of which were expected in nineteenth-century opera. Take them out and you are left with the bare bones of a raw political drama, making it quite different from the overlong and rather diffusely episodic later version. I must say, however, that I rather regret that the Kromy Forest scene was also omitted. It is a magnificent evocation of the chaos and anarchy that were to follow Boris's demise. It completes the cycle of anarchy–order–anarchy that Boris's reign represented in Russian history. However, without the plot developments in the Polish scenes, it is arguable if it makes much dramaturgical sense to include it.

The Boris I had to play for Kupfer was a great strain on my nature. It was a characterisation which was violent, physical, extrovert, hysterical and totally lacking in inner calm. I found it hard to do because it meant unlearning and abandoning the very centred, intense and personal Boris I had developed with Tarkovsky and of which I had become curiously protective. I found the whole process of remaking my own emotional and physical responses to the same music and the same text for a different production seriously unsettling. Too much of that sort of thing could cause real damage to one's mental health. Producers are often very rude about singers' reluctance to rehearse and reconsider roles with which they are very familiar. My own experience is that the process is so painful and puts one under such stress that it is one's self-protective instinct that creates reluctance, not laziness. Certainly Kupfer destroyed my Tarkovsky Boris for ever. I often performed it subsequently in London, St. Petersburg and Vienna, but the personal detail was gone and with Tarkovsky himself dead, there was no way back.[2]

The production which brought me the greatest sense of success with the public and the critics was, perversely, the most romantic and old-fashioned one that I did. That was with Piero Faggioni at the Teatro Communale in Florence. There was, even so, a truly intellectual basis to the production concept, but there is something about the Italians and their idea of opera which makes it impossible to play on an intensely honest dramatic level. They require and expect an 'operatic' dimension to the singing and the playing. We have all been encouraged to sneer at this quality in recent years while we have been in the grip of 'producers' opera. But even if you tried you couldn't entirely avoid it in Italy, because the way the singers sing, the way the chorus performs, the way the orchestra plays, all create a world of heightened projection and consciousness in the audience. Accordingly the Boris I played in Florence was the closest I am prepared to go towards old-fashioned 'ham'.

Faggioni is himself a bit of an old-fashioned 'star'. He was an actor of distinction himself and is accordingly an exceptionally fine acting coach, which is perhaps the most important of the many functions of an opera producer. His talent is to be able to activate under-powered and over-intellectual Anglo-Saxon singers to great vividness of expression and to energise the histrionically reluctant and over voice-conscious Italians to some degree of dramatic urgency. In doing this he creates a chaotic working atmosphere of near hysteria which is utterly exhausting, but ultimately rewarding.

Faggioni is unusual too in that he does his own designs and he lavishes huge amounts of energy on them. Opera is his life, and he is totally preoccupied with

[2] Harry Kupfer's production of "Boris Godunov" was staged in 1986 at the Netherlands Opera with Hartmut Haenchen conducting.

it, in a way that sometimes makes one afraid for his personal health. The designs for Boris were an attempt to represent visually the dark, stubborn and unfathomable quality of Mother Russia. To do it he made casts from real giant redwood trees and lined the stage with them to its full depth. Their huge roots intertwined in the centre of the stage creating a tangled and treacherous surface on which all the chorus scenes took place. The location of each scene was indicated by back projections and cut-out perspective models of St Basil's Cathedral, The Kremlin and so on, seen in the distance. The Court scenes took place on a wooden platform which slid out over the roots. The impression conveyed was that the main characters were strolling players in the eternally immutable life of Russia; players whose moment is soon past and whose impact is depressingly ephemeral. In all this Faggioni expressed very much the essence of Boris as I saw it: his reign was a brief candle quickly swallowed up in the blackness of history.

The personality he gave me for Boris was based on the Eisenstein film of Ivan the Terrible. Boris wore a robe, had long hair, and was youthful looking, almost Messianic, making his extreme violence come as a great surprise. Faggioni could not resist a few 'tricks'. He had me act a heart attack, which coming as it did in mid-flow of Boris's violence against Shuisky, was rather shockingly effective. In fact the first time I did it he thought I really had had an attack, which I thought was praise indeed. He also had me to do a long, slow death fall – not as long as Christoff's but with much the same intention. For me these tricks were never more than tricks. However much the audience liked them, I found them nothing but extraneous devices that detracted from the essence of the character. In this production I never achieved the feeling that I so treasured in the Tarkovsky production of making it up as I went along.[3]

It is impossible to generalise about playing opera from the experience of Boris Godunov. It is a unique experience which I am enormously grateful to have had. Once you have that experience all the old ways of doing opera seem stale and invalid. The repertory system of hastily revived, ill-remembered productions, such as you find in Germany, seem unforgivable. Performances where the singers indulge in generalised gestures and poses, where the chorus stand around looking uncomprehending become intolerable. Playing Boris with the help of these three great producers revealed what all opera could be if we all took the necessary trouble. All of them were prepared to go to infinite lengths in the hope of saying, through the medium of opera, something worth saying. Of course in "Boris Godunov" they had a vehicle worthy of that intention.

The strain of adjusting to these different readings was very considerable. At times I rather envy the old stars who did 'their' performances in the same way everywhere they went. They must have developed a great sense of confidence and certainty. It must have been a great deal more comfortable for them. Their sense of the identity of Boris must have become very strong over the years. My Boris is dead. I have lost him now. I don't know who he is any more. If and when I ever do the opera again I will have to start all over again with a new producer and discover him from scratch. Maybe that's not such a bad thing. If you don't have to do it too often.

---

[3] Piero Faggioni's production of Boris Godunov was staged at the Maggio Musicale Florence in 1988 with Myung Wung Chun conducting.

Musical Performance,
1996, Vol. 1, Part 1, pp. 31–39
Reprints available directly from the publisher
Photocopying permitted by license only

Sir Thomas Beecham: A Memoir

Basil Tschaikov

Sir Thomas Beecham was one of this century's most influential musicians. His inspiration was felt internationally, but particularly in Britain where he revolutionised standards and attitudes in the orchestra and opera house, profoundly affecting public taste and expectations in performance. At the same time, he was a most unconventional conductor and artist, whose unique methods and approach have mystified some writers. The author of this memoir played for Sir Thomas regularly in the clarinet sections of the London Philharmonic and Royal Philharmonic Orchestras from the time this remarkable conductor returned to his old orchestra (the LPO) in 1944, after two years absence in the Americas, and then in the RPO from 1947 until Sir Thomas's final concert in 1960.

A small man with a little white beard walked majestically towards the platform, followed – at a respectful distance – by his wife, his manager, the orchestra's general manager and concert manager, and one or two others. He came onto the platform and took his place on the podium. "Good morning! It is very good to be back with you again. Let us begin with the Berlioz overture – *Carnaval Romain.*" Those few words of greeting were the first I heard in that rich, plummy Edwardian voice, with its inimitable inflection.

It was the 30th September 1944, and we were in Wembley Town Hall. Sir Thomas Beecham had just arrived back in Britain from the Americas where he had been since 1940. He had returned to rejoin his old orchestra, the London Philharmonic, and this was to be their first rehearsal. It was also my first experience of the great man.

I had often listened to those wonderful recordings he had made between 1932 and 1939 with the pre-war LPO, but it had never occurred to me that I might have the incredible good fortune to play under his direction at all, let alone so soon, at the tender age of nineteen.

It was well known that Sir Thomas was frequently late, but this time he exceeded even his own reputation – he was three weeks late. On this occasion the orchestra awaited his arrival with some anxiety. It was still war-time and his voyage across the Atlantic would be long and dangerous. The tension in the orchestra mounted whilst we waited for his return and now everyone was keyed up.

Perhaps he felt he must show that he had not changed his habits whilst away from Britain; on the morning of our first rehearsal with him he was over an hour late. But, after those first few words of greeting and a swift glance round the orchestra, up went the baton and we were off.

Though I had already played with a number of fine conductors I knew at once that this was something special. The *Allegro* at the start of the Overture was so alive and vibrant and the slow section that follows, though still taut rhythmically, had the flexible lyricism that I came to learn was characteristic of this remarkable conductor. Then back into the *allegro* six-eight again. With mounting excitement we approached the main theme. Just when the first *allegro* melody returns there is a big accent. At that moment an astonishing thing happened – Beecham gave a great lunge, to emphasise the accent, and stuck the baton through his left hand. It went right through and came out the other side.

So, after only about five minutes' rehearsal he was rushed off to the hospital. He returned for the afternoon rehearsal, his left hand bandaged and in a sling, but otherwise his usual ebullient self.

This was the first occasion I played for Beecham, but I had heard about Sir Thomas from my father, also a clarinettist. He played for Beecham in the short-lived, but adventurous Beecham Wind Orchestra in 1912. Later he played for Sir Thomas, several times, in various orchestras. As a child I remember him speaking of these occasions with enthusiasm.

I also knew the wonderful records Beecham had made with the London Philharmonic Orchestra between 1932 and 1939; some of his leading players – Reginald Kell, Leon Goosens, Anthony Pini and David MacCallum, had been my boyhood heroes. I loved the way one heard the woodwind solos so clearly; the players always seemed to have such freedom of expression and the opportunity to be creative. I was to learn later, from personal experience, that when playing for Sir Thomas one never had to fight one's way through a barrage of strings, 'scraping away regardless', as Sir Henry Wood used to call it, when playing a soft, delicate solo passage.

Beecham formed the LPO in 1932 and from the start he and the orchestra were a great success. The audience at the first concert were stunned and excited by the verve and virtuosity of the performance of the very first item *Carnaval Romain Overture*, by Berlioz, one of Beecham's favourite works. Recently I had the opportunity of hearing the views of some of the players who had played with him during the thirties, when he was younger than I ever knew him.

Richard Walton, his principal trumpet, recalled that "he had authority – and he used that authority. He could be quite a tartar. It had to be really good." Leo Birnbaum, one of the violas, remembers the excitement of working with Tommy. "He was one of those few rare conductors who could really get better playing out of us than other conductors. At the first rehearsal Tommy would conduct the whole work, straight through. He'd get excited and we'd get excited, too. At the end we'd all cheer. I think that sometimes these rehearsals were even more exciting, to us, than the actual performance. Even after the last rehearsal he'd be busy with his blue pencil, putting in what we call 'hairpins' – crescendos and diminuendos – he was always marking and re-marking nuances."

Richard Walton and I played together in the Royal Philharmonic, Tommy's last orchestra, and knew his blue pencil marks well. This could be a sore trial for his librarian, George Brownfoot. Quite often George and the composer Leonard Salzedo, then a violinist in the RPO, would be marking the individual parts of a piece we were to play in the second half of the concert whilst we were playing the first half.

We had both experienced the excitement of his rehearsal style. But, as Walton put it, "He always implied a lyrical line – I'm sure both the orchestras, the LPO and RPO, had this from Beecham – the importance of a beautiful, lyrical line. Sometimes he would smile, not at anyone in particular, but just because it was coming off as he wished – what he was searching for was there." During my years with Beecham I was to hear that beautiful lyrical line many times, and see the smile of pleasure on his face when we responded to his wishes.

Whilst Beecham was in the Americas the LPO had become self-managed, electing its own Directors from the members of the orchestra. It was inevitable that Beecham's autocratic nature and his need for total artistic control, and the democratic structure of the LPO management would soon lead to a confrontation. After about a year Tommy and the LPO parted company. Before long, in 1946, he formed his last great orchestra, the Royal Philharmonic (Figure 1), with whom he was to have a long and successful relationship until his death in 1961.

In 1947 I was fortunate to have the opportunity of joining that orchestra, at the same time as clarinettist Jack Brymer. I was reviving old memories with Jack recently and remembering some of the works we had played many times with Tommy. I recalled how different his rehearsal methods were from other conductors. Jack Brymer responded with his own recollections. "His rehearsals were more a matter of familiarization than anything else. You went there – you hadn't the faintest idea what the old man wanted, really, because he didn't put it into words. But when you got to the performance you looked at him, you looked at those eyes and the whole body, and the gestures, and you knew what he wanted, because this was real conducting, the art of gesture. I remember one day, he had just returned from America, and he said, 'Let's see what we can do with this little bit of music.' and we played *On Hearing The First Cuckoo in Spring*, by Delius. If you listen to that recording – fantastic – it is affection in music." And indeed it is. I think it was experiences like that which had such a great influence on all those who had the privilege of making music with him. It has always seemed to me that I could tell, from their playing, whoever happened to be conducting, those musicians who had played for Tommy for any length of time. Whatever their individual ability one heard traces of the lyricism, rubato, and freedom of expression, that were the hall-marks of a Beecham performance.

However many times you played a piece – perhaps the Mozart symphony No. 39 in E♭, which I must have played dozens of times with him – he always rehearsed it again. His method of rehearsal was to say, "Now then, shall we have a look at the Mozart symphony, please?" After we had played right through to the end, without any stops, he would usually say, "Yes, that was very nice, gentlemen." and I would say to my friend Jack Brymer, "That means we're going through it again." Then Tommy would say, "Just one or two points – it's going extremely well." – and we'd go straight through the whole piece again.

But, of course, we didn't *just play* through it again, because he would do different things with the baton, he would look in a different way, his gestures would change. He knew what he wanted to hear, he knew what had not gone the way he wished and he would do what was needed, in some subtle extraordinary way, that enabled the players to produce the sounds he heard in his head and wanted to hear from the orchestra.

He didn't tell you what to do, or explain it. He used to say "You don't have to teach musicians – they're good musicians – they probably know more about the music than you do. All that you can do is help them play that music together, come together to make a performance."

I think it was at his seventy-fifth birthday party that he said, "As I get older I've learnt to do less and less." Some people might think that he didn't really mean it,

Figure 1 Sir Thomas Beecham – a photograph taken whilst he was music director of the Royal Philharmonic Orchestra.

but it was absolutely true. Tommy did do less and less, that is he got in the way less and less. He conducted like a man bowling a hoop along. He tapped the hoop only when it was necessary. When he came to a corner he tapped it so that it started to go round and left it alone until it had gone round. Then he tapped it again. Others tap it all the way round the corner, and as likely as not it goes into the wall.

No other conductor, that I have known, was able to get an orchestra to play with such a degree of rubato and yet, at the same time, achieve outstanding precision of attack and ensemble. There was something so inevitable in his rhythm, that however wayward his beat might appear, you always knew what was happening.

In the 1947 recording of *Ein Heldenleben*, by Richard Strauss, there are some wonderful examples of this talent. In particular, towards the end of that work where there is a lovely duet between the violin and the horn that is of breathtaking loveliness (on that record it is played with great sensitivity by the then Leader, Oscar Lampe and the late, great Dennis Brain). It was taking part in performances like that, when Tommy combined masculine tenderness, subtle rubato, sensitive phrasing and dynamic outbursts of energy, that made working with him something very special indeed.

But Sir Thomas was a man of many sides and moods – as all great artists seem to be. On the occasion of a concert in which *Ein Heldenleben* was to feature, Dennis Brain, an artist with a considerable solo career as well as his orchestral commitments, had already accepted an engagement to play one of the Mozart horn concertos with another orchestra. He told the orchestral manager he would not be available for the concert. Beecham said, "Either Mr Brain makes himself available for our concert, or he will not play with the orchestra again." Dennis Brain did not do the concert and did not play in the orchestra again. Brain was one of Sir Thomas's favourite players, yet he would let him go rather than have his authority challenged.

Notwithstanding his autocratic style, Beecham was always popular with musicians. Though his public image was that he was a martinet and very authoritarian he was always called 'Tommy', by the musicians who worked for him, when they spoke of him to each other. And nearly always with affection. His reputation for off-the-cuff humour is not something that I experienced to any extent. His tone of voice, choice of words, and manner of speaking often led to quite ordinary remarks being greeted with howls of laughter. He could make 'pass the salt' sound amusing.

I suspect that some of his more famous asides and ripostes had been contrived previously and, perhaps, honed, ready for use when required. But it may be that it was when he was younger (he was already 65 when I first played for him) that he coined his most remembered retorts.

One occasion when it must have been spontaneous was when my father played for Sir Thomas for the first time in about 1910 or 1911, as deputy principal clarinet in one of the orchestras Sir Thomas was conducting. In the course of the rehearsal Beecham, wishing to make some musical point to my father and not knowing his name, turned to the principal second violinist and asked him "who is playing principal clarinet today?" Unfortunately this player suffered from a quite dreadful stutter. "It's Mr Tch – Tch – Tch. Tchhhh. . . . ." "Oh! dear!" said Sir Thomas, "Do we have a train with us today?"

Of course, he provided a great deal of employment, paid well, and from time to time put a considerable amount of his own money, as well as other people's, into his musical enterprises. But that was not the main thing. It was, as always, the pleasure that nearly all musicians got from taking part in magical performances that make the difficult and sometimes unrewarding life of an orchestral musician really worthwhile.

For many years Beecham had wanted to take an orchestra to the USA. In 1950 after several attempts, a tour was finally organized and we set off across the Atlantic on the old Queen Mary. It was a lengthy, tiring trip, lasting from September until December, involving a great deal of travelling and fifty-six concerts.

After a fortnight of concerts in New England, including Boston and Washington, we played two concerts in New York in Carnegie Hall. Our first concert had been in Hartford, Connecticut, which we had been told would be our 'blooding'. If this concert was well received by the critics (who would travel up from New York), the concerts we were to give in Carnegie Hall would be well received. Otherwise we could expect a rough reception in New York – especially as Beecham had for years boasted of the superiority of his British orchestras.

The conditions on the luxury liner, in contrast to the semi-wartime conditions prevailing in Britain – where food and clothing were still rationed – were extremely agreeable. But good food, an abundance of alcohol, and no opportunity for practice for a week, did little for playing standards. Added to this the orchestra had taken on a number of extra players, some of whom were unfamiliar with the repertoire.

The first rehearsal in the afternoon in Hartford, preceding the evening concert, got off to a bad start. A number of the principals arrived late having been delayed for some reason. Sir Thomas, nearly always late himself, was on this occasion ready and waiting and quickly became angry at being unable to start on time.

When the orchestra was eventually assembled it sounded extremely rough. Out of tune, poor ensemble, and lacking in dynamics or finesse. Had I been in Beecham's place I think I would have considered a hasty retreat back home. But that was not Tommy's style.

When we arrived at the concert it was with some apprehension. There was a buzz of expectancy from the audience as we took our places on the platform and tuned up. Sir Thomas walked on in his usual slow and dignified manner; he raised the baton and in a moment, with a tremendous downward swipe, started the National Anthem. It was done with such courage and passion that it raised the spirit of the whole orchestra in an extraordinary way, inspiring and enthusing everyone. The concert went extremely well, we received good notices, and began the tour in high spirits.

We played in major cities: New Orleans, Chicago, Detroit, Philadelphia, and a great many smaller towns and Universities before arriving back in New York again for our final concerts.

Throughout Tommy was in fine form – amazing for a man of his age (most of the orchestra found it very hard going at times). One Southern critic called him 'The Great Little Metrognome!' He was not at all pleased, preferring to jest at others' expense rather than being on the receiving end.

Beecham liked to rescue music that had been neglected, perhaps deservedly, or because it required someone with his special kind of imagination to bring it to life. One such work that I enjoyed very much, to which Tommy brought his magic, was *Fifine at the Fair* by Granville Bantock. This employs a very large orchestra, in the Strauss/Mahler tradition. Though rather too long it has some fine dramatic moments and lyrical interludes, which Beecham realised to their full potential.

Goldmark's *Rustic Wedding Symphony*, surely deserving of more performances, was another of Tommy's favourites. In the recording he made, with the RPO, the slow movement is played with particular sensitivity and beauty of tone colouring. One hears the lyrical, firm yet infinitely flexible rhythm Beecham brought to everything he conducted. The music moves forward, never dragging, always unhurried and timeless.

Another favourite of his, *The Last Sleep of the Virgin*, by Massenet, usually consigned to the 'lollipop' category, is a little gem. When I heard it last, in Sir Thomas's own beautifully shaped recording, on the occasion of his re-burial, only a few yards away from his beloved Delius, in the little churchyard of St. Peter's, Limpsfield, it was also intensely moving.[1]

His championship of Delius is well known and his recordings of the very large works, *The Mass of Life*, *A Village Romeo and Juliet*, *Irmelin* and many smaller works remain as the touchstone for performance of these great compositions. The sounds he drew from the orchestra were transparent and airy, supported by an extraordinary rhythmic spine that moves the music along, never letting it become shapeless, as it can be in other hands.

I remember very clearly the week of performances of Delius' *Irmelin* which were given in Oxford. This was a real act of heroism on Beecham's part. The staging was somewhat primitive (some said the previous year's *Cinderella* scenery was used!), audiences were rather thin and the takings at the box office resulted in a very large deficit, which took a very long time to pay off. For me, at least, it was worthwhile for the wonderful music. No doubt it would benefit from some cuts, but there is so much of outstanding beauty that one waits for more performances – but, without Beecham will it ever be the same?

Though Beecham was an innovator for a large part of his life he showed little sympathy for music written after 1940. Nonetheless his programmes were extremely varied. He loved French music: Cesar Franck, Saint-Saëns, Bizet – a great favourite of Beecham's was the symphony (a minor masterpiece, far too seldom performed) – Massenet, Debussy and occasionally Ravel.

The performance of Ravel's Daphnis and Chloe Suite No 2, at a Royal Festival Hall concert, remains as a memory of what, in other hands, would have been a major catastrophe. Notwithstanding his wonderful sense of rhythm, Tommy had no liking for 5/4 or 7/8 time signatures. He was frightened of the 5/4 section towards the end of Daphnis and Chloe and therefore barely rehearsed it. At the concert one player, with an important solo entry, came in a bar early. Some sections of the orchestra followed him, some did not. Beecham bellowed and wagged the baton frenetically, under the conductor's stand. Gradually the music fell apart; at one point I think only the two flutes were still 'wiffling' away. But the orchestra rallied and we finished together, always an asset. "How about that for a near disaster?" I said to the conductor Norman Del Mar, when I saw him after the concert. "Well," he said, "it was a bit untidy in one place, but, my goodness, what an exciting and splendid performance!"

---

1 On 29 April 1991.

As well as Richard Strauss, Sibelius, Tchaikovsky and regular performances of his beloved Mozart, and to a lesser extent Haydn, we played a good deal of Brahms and Beethoven. Beecham is sometimes thought to have ignored the German masterpieces. This was not so. Brahms' second symphony and the St. Anthony Variations were regularly in his programmes, and the other symphonies rather less frequently. We often played Beethoven's second, fourth and sixth symphonies. The Pastoral was rather slower than usual, but the second and fourth were the best renditions of these works that I can recall. He also liked the seventh symphony which we played quite frequently. The Ninth symphony was scheduled several times, but for some reason Beecham seemed to be heir to ill-health on most of these occasions and his place was taken by someone else.

Tommy was a conductor who needed to be musically 'in charge'. He was a wonderful accompanist, within the framework of his own conception. For players and singers who shared his view of a work he was a delightful collaborator. Soloists with a similar degree of individuality could be less happy.

His recordings of *Magic Flute*, *Carmen* and *La Boheme*, are ample evidence of his powers as an opera conductor. On the concert platform he used soloists rather infrequently. I recall an outstanding performance with Cifford Curzon, who put his subtle artistry at Beecham's disposal in a magnificent reading of Brahms' second piano concerto. There were a number of performances of the Sibelius violin concerto with Isaac Stern, who also made a splendid recording of this work with Tommy. The recording of the Mendelssohn violin concerto with Jascha Heifetz was a less happy occasion. At one point it seemed unlikely that the recording would ever be completed satisfactorily. Heifetz had decided that he wanted to play the last movement extremely quickly. Certainly much faster than Sir Thomas was inclined to think correct. Heifetz played at one tempo, Beecham conducted at another. The rest of us, in particular the woodwind, had to do the best we could. The result is interesting, if not quite orthodox.

When we travelled to Portsmouth in May 1960, it never occurred to any of us that this would be the last concert that Sir Thomas would conduct. He was in good shape and it seemed he would go on for ever. We all hoped he would. As on the occasion when I first encountered Sir Thomas – when he put the baton through his hand – this concert also was to have strange and unusual events connected with it.

For some reason he had decided to invite the whole orchestra to luncheon before the rehearsal in Portsmouth. This was extremely unusual, indeed unique in my experience. Though always polite and courteous, Beecham never became familiar with members of his orchestras. He neither travelled with the players nor indulged in any kind of social relationship with them. However, this was a very pleasant occasion and Tommy was at his most benign. After lunch we went to the concert hall and rehearsed for about twenty minutes. Then another surprise. A large television set was brought on to the platform and Sir Thomas invited the orchestra to join him in watching the cup-final. The team from his hometown, Liverpool, was playing that year. There was no more rehearsal and after the match we went our separate ways.

It was a splendid concert and it was received with enthusiasm. Our first encore was *The Dance of the Priestesses* from *Samson and Delilah* by Saint-Saëns. Tommy was loved by audiences and he in his turn loved them and was generous with his encores. He loved music and enjoyed it more than any other conductor I have played for. It was this enjoyment that was so infectious, affecting audiences and players alike.

Shirley, Lady Beecham told me that Tommy had related to her how on an occasion, when he was very, very young, there was a little concert in his hometown at which he was to play the piano. He was terrified of the audience. His nurse led him to the curtain and let him peep through. "Now, Master Thomas, you mustn't be nervous" she said "out there are all your little friends". On this occasion, in Portsmouth, a great many of his friends, in the audience and all of us on the platform, were treated to another encore, a characteristically ebullient performance of *The Bacchanale*, also from *Samson and Delilah*. It was the last piece he was to conduct.

The treasury of incomparable commercial recordings that Sir Thomas has left to enrich the listening hours of all music lovers is testimony to his remarkable range of musical sympathies. From Handel, Haydn, Mozart, and Schubert, to Strauss, Delius, and Sibelius, by way of Beethoven, Brahms, Tchaikovsky and Dvorak; Berlioz, Bizet, Massenet, Saint-Saëns, Offenbach, and Chabrier; and then those composers often neglected – Bantock, Goldmark, Busoni, and Ponchielli.

Readers who can visit the Music Performance Research Centre's Listening Studio at the Barbican Centre can also enjoy a number of archive-recordings of Beecham performances that cannot be heard elsewhere, including the *Grande Messe des Morts* by Berlioz, with Rene Soames, Choruses and the BBC Symphony Orchestra (1947); the Busoni Piano Concerto, played by Noel Mewton-Wood with the BBC Symphony Orchestra (1948); *A Village Romeo and Juliet* by Delius, with Soloists, Chorus, and the Royal Philharmonic Orchestra (1948); Dvorak's Symphony No 5, with the London Philharmonic Orchestra (1936).

But for those of us, like myself, who were fortunate enough to enjoy and be inspired by making music with this unique musician there is a gap that can never be filled.

Musical Performance,
1996, Vol. 1, Part 1, pp. 41–55
Reprints available directly from the publisher
Photocopying permitted by license only

A View from the Orchestra – Two Perspectives

Harold Nash and David Theodore

Performing musicians are often asked how they became professionals, and what their lives in music are like, especially by students who are aspiring professionals. The answers inevitably vary greatly. In the case of orchestral artists, people are sometimes surprised that such an integrated ensemble as an orchestra can comprise musicians whose backgrounds and careers can differ very considerably. Harold Nash and David Theodore are successful and distinguished musicians in London. Though they come from different generations and their careers have taken rather different paths, there was a time when they were both principals in the Royal Opera Orchestra, Covent Garden, for several years; Nash as principal trombone – he joined the orchestra in 1956 and is still the resident principal, and Theodore as principal oboe from 1982 until 1987.

Nash in his interview and Theodore in his article each describe the route by which they entered the profession, the differing skills and responsibilities demanded depending on the music performed and the type of orchestra, and the considerable changes that have taken place in the British orchestral profession over the past 30 years.

In describing their careers they remember some of the celebrated artists with whom they have performed.

I. Harold Nash in Conversation with Jon Tolansky

Harold Nash began his career with one of Britain's leading brass bands, Parc and Dare Workman's Band, in the 1940s, in the days when many of the UK's finest brass players were weaned in the numerous mining colliery bands that have nearly all now disappeared. He became a member of Sir Thomas Beecham's Royal Philharmonic Orchestra in 1950; in 1952 took up the post of principal trombone in the Sadlers Wells Opera. In 1956 he was invited by the Royal Opera's music director, Rafael Kubelik, to join the Orchestra of the Royal Opera House, Covent Garden. Since then he has also played from time to time with the four London orchestra (London Philharmonic, London Symphony, Philharmonia, Royal Philharmonic) and with other organisations including the Philip Jones Brass Ensemble and the National Philharmonic Orchestra, a recording group. From 1981 to 1992 he was head of brass at the Royal Academy of Music.

JT: Why did you chose to play the trombone?

HN: It wasn't a deliberate choice – it happened by accident. My father, who was a keen brass band man was teaching another young chap and I got a little bit jealous. "Why can you teach other boys and you can't be bothered to teach me?" "All right", he said, "I'll get you a tenor horn". But I didn't get on too well with that so they eventually switched me to the trombone to see if I'd do any better on that.

My father insisted on me practicing every morning before leaving for school, and then again in the evening, before I started doing my homework – the trombone was everything as far as he was concerned. Before long I was in trouble with my headmaster for being late for school too frequently. I was called into his room and he asked me what was the cause of my lateness. "Well", I said, "my father makes me practice the trombone every morning,

I get interested and go on for too long". He then asked me if I thought I could earn my living by playing. When I told him that I didn't know if I could but I'd like to try, he said, "All right. We'll see what you can do".

He got an application form for a scholarship from the Royal Academy of Music and, in due course, I was on my way to London to audition for a place at the Academy. In fact I was awarded the Henderson Scholarship, which is for bassoon, horn, or trombone. At that time I was 15, but only looked about 12, as I was rather small for my age and I think that was one reason for my success.

The other reason was that the Principal and Warden seemed to find my performance very amusing. I played an arrangement of an aria from Gounod's Queen of Sheba. Each time I had a few bars rest I blew the water out of the instrument. After the second or third time this happened they were laughing out loud. I think this, rather than any musical excellence, got me the scholarship.

JT: Was your father a professional musician?

HN: No, he was a coal miner – he'd started working down the mines when he was only 12, but the day before I was born, in 1931, the mine was closed and he was thrown out of work. He was unemployed for most of my childhood and it was only through his connection with the Salvation Army that he finally got a job. His bandmaster had invented a fruit drink that became very successful. He eventually had a number of depots throughout the Welsh Valleys and needed men to take the carts with their great Shire horses round the villages selling his 'pop'. Many of the younger men had joined the forces – this was 1939 – and that helped get my father the job. But what he was really passionately interested in were the Salvation Army Bands – brass bands. So much so that he became the Young People's Bandleader.

JT: Were you interested in orchestral or operatic music at that time?

HN: My first orchestral experience was at school. As it was wartime there was a shortage of staff so we had no music teacher. There was one boy, John Newman, who played the viola and was talented – later he became a County Music Adviser. He found there were a number of boys who could play a bit. One played clarinet, another saxophone; there was also a cellist and quite a good pianist. With John playing viola and me on trombone, he made an arrangement of the Tchaikovsky First Piano Concerto!

It was great fun, I thought that all orchestral playing was going to be like that. Playing all the horn cues and missing parts, playing all the time, was much more fun than playing the actual parts written for the trombone where there are so many bars rest. Then, in 1945, the first National Youth Orchestra in Europe was started in Wales, with Clarence Raybould, who also conducted the Royal Academy of Music orchestra, in charge. He had been one of the BBC staff conductors.

It was amazing! There had been no orchestra at all and then suddenly a whole lot of very talented young musicians appeared. A good many went on to have successful careers as professional musicians – principals in the big orchestras. Derek James to the London Philharmonic Orchestra, Geoffrey Gambold as first bassoon in the BBC Symphony Orchestra, Pat Strevens, horn, in the Philharmonia and Osian Ellis, the very distinguished harpist – soloist, the harpist for many years in the London Symphony Orchestra. If you counted all the musicians who came out of that orchestra over the years it would be quite staggering.

I was in that orchestra for five years, three before I went to the Academy. In fact, I think it may have been that Raybould put in a good word for me and that was why I got the scholarship.

JT: After all that experience in the Welsh Youth Orchestra how valuable were the opportunities available at the Academy?

HN: Practically nil! Raybould tended to do the things that he liked and spent a lot of time on the strings, where there were a lot of girls – he liked to flirt with them a bit. We'd have six days of rehearsal on one programme and then do a concert – it was all rather a waste of time.

JT: So what do you think you got out of your years at the Academy?

HN: In a word – Sidney Langston. He was my trombone teacher. I was extremely fortunate to meet someone like that – he taught me everything. Not just the trombone. He made it clear that was only a minor part of life. I was completely raw, completely green – up from the Welsh Valleys. He taught me how to cope with everything. He encouraged me and became a surrogate father. And because he found my playing satisfactory he was able to give me work as well.

JT: At that time did you have an ambition to become a member of one of the major orchestras?

HN: I don't think I looked that far ahead. I was content just to get through the course and try and play better and better and hope at the end of it I would get a job of some kind. With my background I knew I must work, get a job of some sort. I didn't know if this was going to be teaching or playing. Actually, I was too frightened to look at it too closely.

In the event I was extremely fortunate. Sid Langston, who was principal trombone in the Royal Philharmonic Orchestra, had started putting a few engagements my way. Then the second trombone position in the Royal Philharmonic became vacant. Langston started by trying all the professionals who were available until he got down to me.

"He gave me one date – a live television transmission of *School For Fathers* by Wolf-Ferrari, with John Lanchbery conducting. The Royal Philharmonic Orchestra was up in the top studio and the singers, acting out the opera, were in Studio 1, downstairs. And Jack trying to hold it all together. After that I got one or two more dates with the orchestra followed by a tour with Beecham and Isaac Stern, who made his debut in this country on that tour, playing the Sibelius violin concerto – in Birmingham – and it was terrific. Beecham seemed quite happy with me, so I continued there."

JT: Straight from a background that was tough and difficult into the RPO. Almost fresh out of college into one of the most prestigious orchestras in the world, Sir Thomas Beecham's newly formed, last and, perhaps, greatest orchestra. How did you react to that?

HN: I don't think I did react – I didn't really take it in. I was obviously worried about keeping the job, doing what Sid Langston wanted and playing properly.

Probably the reason he liked having me there was because I listened and learnt from him, tried to play like him, which is maybe why it was successful.

JT: There were a number of individual and powerful principals in the orchestra at that time. They not only influenced their own sections, but the orchestra as a whole. Was Langston one of these and did he have a big influence on you?

HN: Sid was in the same position as the other principals, he was responsible for picking the players (and getting rid of them!) for his own section. There had been several second trombones before I settled there. That tour had actually been an audition – he had the power to decide, but, of course, Beecham had the last word. If Beecham hadn't liked it I wouldn't have been there.

JT: What was it like for you? Sir Thomas was a very individual, one-off kind of conductor, and though you were obviously extremely talented you had had very little experience?

HN: It was surprisingly easy. Even at that stage I didn't feel nervous with him. He didn't make the orchestra nervous because he smiled and encouraged everyone.

JT: Yes. Most musicians who worked with Beecham said this. He enabled you to enjoy yourself in a way no-one else did. He had high standards, but he never achieved them in a destructive way.

HN: No – I don't remember him ever glaring at anyone, even when things went wrong. No fuss whatsoever.

JT: He knew what he wanted.

HN: Oh yes. He didn't have to say anything – you knew. And even questions of intonation in, say, Delius – which is notoriously difficult to tune – he would turn round to Terry Macdonagh, the principal oboe, and say "Oh! Mr Macdonagh would you give us an 'A' please". And Terry would, and the other woodwind players and others would tune up, and we'd carry on. He'd never say "You're sharp", or "You're flat", or complain.

JT: You remained with the orchestra for about three years?

HN: Yes.

JT: Did that experience have a powerful influence on your life?

HN: I regret that I wasn't mature enough to appreciate it. I was terribly young. I didn't really understand what I was doing or what it was all about. It was just a matter of coping with the job and enjoying it – and being very chuffed with the whole thing. But I wish I'd been more mature.

JT: How do you feel now when you hear some of the recordings you made 40 years ago? Do you feel 'That was us?' That orchestra had a unique style of playing – probably because of the very special relationship that developed between Beecham and the musicians in the RPO at that time.

HN: Strangely, the feeling I have – if I'm playing any of those pieces, or listening to them – is that I don't hear what's actually going on. I hear what happened then; I'm there in an idealised performance. Meistersinger overture – how many times must I have played it since then? – but I always hear Beecham's version which was totally different from anybody else's. Unforgettable!

JT: Why did you leave the RPO?

HN: In 1952, the Sadlers Wells orchestra was reformed and a good many younger players were recruited. I was one of them. By this time I felt I had learnt a lot from Sid Langston; I wanted to play like him but I couldn't do that in a second trombone job. I wanted to be a first trombonist, to lead, have a say in things. I asked Sid what he thought and he said he thought it would do me the world of good. I did the audition and got the job – really terrific.

JT: And from there you went on to the Royal Opera House Orchestra?

HN: Again I was very lucky, as I've been most of my life. Rafael Kubelik came along to conduct *Katya Kabanova* – it was a tremendous experience. Shortly after we had done *Katya* with him for the second time the trombone position at Covent Garden became vacant, rather suddenly, and they wanted someone to come in to share the principal trombone position. Kubelik recommended me to the orchestra manager at the Garden, Morris Smith, who as it happens had been a trombonist himself. He came to hear a performance of the *Magic Flute* which has quite a good part for the trombone – it was a sort of audition. The next morning he phoned and asked me to come to Covent Garden to discuss a contract.

It all happened so fast and, of course, I was delighted, but also a bit concerned. At that time there was a good deal of rivalry between the teachers at the Royal College of Music and the Royal Academy. Morris Smith was the professor at the College and Sidney Langston at the Academy. They didn't speak to each other and certainly didn't engage each other's pupils. I thought

"I've only got this job because they're in a jam. In a year's time he'll put one of his pupils in". But, after 39 years I'm still there!

JT: What was the difference between the two schools of playing?

HN: Well they were and still continue, to some extent, to be two distinct schools. I've tried to carry on the Langston tradition, but there have been very fine players produced by both traditions. My school of playing is, I think, more direct, more French in a way. The start and end of each note is clearly defined and tends to be shortish. More operatic, perhaps. The other school is more modern sounding – very soft and mellow in approach – you don't hear the note start or end. More Germanic.

JT: Isn't that sort of distinction, coming from dominant players, rather less now?

HN: I'm afraid it is. The trombone has become a machine, like a Yamaha Keyboard. It plays all the notes and is safe: This is more the College style of playing and maybe scores, because it's safer. There's much more mixing between the two camps now. I like to think that by going to the Garden, where I was the stranger in Morris' camp I helped to break the mould.

JT: When you went to the Opera House in 1956 Kubelik had just joined as the music director and Covent Garden was moving towards becoming one of the very finest opera houses. How did you find being in the orchestra at that time?

HN: It was certainly exciting. It was a real Company then, not as it has become now, when conductors and singers come and go on a seasonal basis. Sometimes singers sing with conductors they've not worked with before. We still have our own chorus and our own orchestra, but that is virtually the only musical stability these days. And of course we had Kubelik who was there all the time. He lived in his little flat upstairs – he was there throughout the year. There was no jetsetting – he conducted something like seven or eight operas every season, and they were big operas, Parsifal, Tristan, etc. Every season. That's something we don't see from the music director these days.

JT: So you had a real relationship with him?

HN: Absolutely. He was a father figure – you could talk to him and he knew everyone and similarly with the singers. Joan Carlyle, Edgar Evans, Joan Sutherland – and many other fine singers – they were singing in most things. The finest thing I heard Joan Sutherland sing was Micaela in Carmen – that was before she became such a clever singer. It was totally innocent and wonderful, just right for that part.

JT: Did the singers and the orchestra meet socially?

HN: Yes – to a great extent because we went on tour. There was at least one tour every year which lasted 10 or 12 weeks. We nearly always went to the Edinburgh Festival – that would have been another four weeks. So there was that sort of contact. The company was smaller and we met one another in the canteen. Nowadays the canteen is much bigger and there are so many more employees that one doesn't know, so orchestra and singers tend to keep to themselves.

JT: And the personnel in the orchestra – were there many changes?

HN: Players stayed a long time, and of course some are still there. Morris Smith used to say, "In this orchestra either you stay one season, two at the most, and you leave; or you stay forever".

JT: Did a real tradition of performing develop at the Opera House?

HN: Absolutely. Sad to say I don't think it's still there. The turnover is far greater now – the orchestra certainly feels much younger to me – and, of course, we have virtually two orchestras. I'm not sure that is a good idea musically. It used to be that more or less the same section met on each occasion. Now when you arrive for a performance you don't know who is going to be sitting next to you! And that's happening throughout the orchestra so you don't get the same cohesion that you did in the past.

When I first started at the opera house we were getting such good training – Kubelik was a tremendously good trainer, he was so reliable. Then there was John Pritchard. In my opinion he was technically the best conductor I think I have played for, especially in the 19th-century 'coloratura' repertory. No one can conduct those operas like John – and he did it so casually. He made it look so easy.

JT: What was it like when Giulini made his debut in 1958?

HN: Amazing! He produced a real Italian style of playing from the orchestra. We had had Italian conductors, Erede, Serafin, and others, but they were from the old school. Giulini had all that tradition but with a modern technique for putting it across.

Recently, when Gwyneth Jones was singing in Fanciulla, I was reminded of when she sang in Il Trovatore with Giulini. The staggering thing is that I haven't heard her sing as well to this day as she did then, with him. It just shows what a great influence a man like Giulini can have. He was able to raise Gwyneth so far above herself – and she was already a wonderful singer – and inspire her, and the orchestra, too, by just being there, standing on the rostrum.

Too often the rehearsals can be boring because they are really for the conductor. The orchestra and the singers know the music but the conductor doesn't – he doesn't know quite how to pull it all together. As he gets more and more tense it gets worse. That never happens with really fine conductors. I remember when Carlos Kleiber came to conduct Boheme in 1979. Rehearsals were never boring and one heard it getting better and better –

but, then, he's an outstanding exception. Too often the more rehearsal time they have the worse it gets. Sometimes a repetiteur will have to take over a performance, already prepared by a conductor who has fallen ill, without any rehearsal. And it goes very well, and so does the next performance. On the next occasion he is given several rehearsals – and we realise how indifferent he is!

JT: In 1959 Solti made his debut with Der Rosenkavalier, and then stayed for 11 years. How important was that?

HN: Oh, very important. He was very good for our morale. We had been through rather a rough period after Kubelik left and although we had some good guest conductors we didn't have a captain at the helm. Morale was a bit low because we kept hearing rumours about who was going to be the next musical director, and then nothing happened. For a time there was a battle between Kempe and Giulini – not personally – but it was Webster's[1] idea to have them both, one for the German repertoire and the other for the Italian. Of course, neither would agree to that. They both wanted to be completely in charge. So we were glad when Solti was chosen.

We had already worked with him – we had done some recording sessions of ballet music – so we knew what to expect. We were rather frightened, actually, because he was terribly demanding. He had a good effect on the orchestra – we all had to make sure we could play the impossible for him! We had to work hard because the orchestra became a star with him. Whatever was going on, on stage, seemed to come second – the star was down there on the rostrum, and we were with him. Whether this was always the right thing musically was questioned. A good many singers didn't enjoy singing for him because they felt the orchestra was too loud and he and the orchestra were getting too much attention.

Quite a few people didn't like his Ring – they found it too harsh. Maybe the reason was because he was trying to reproduce the sound of the Decca recording he had made – and that's a wonderful recording. But it doesn't really sound like the Rings we did before, or since.

Nevertheless, there were also a lot of good things – the extraordinary combination of Erwartung, L'Heure Espagnol and Il Tabarro, all in one evening's performance. They were tremendous, and so was Britten's Midsummer Night's Dream. Perhaps his greatest triumph with us was Schoenberg's Moses and Aaron which I think was under-valued.

JT: It's now 1994 – how do you feel about the 1970s, after Solti left? Can you give some idea of the changes you have seen and heard over the last 25 years, and your feeling about being at this world-famous opera house for so many years?

HN: When Colin Davis came I liked him, and he did a lot of things extremely well – he covered almost the entire repertoire, and did most of it

[1] Sir David Webster, General Administrator, the Royal Opera House Covent Garden, 1946 to 1970.

very well. The Ring got much better – the last Ring he did went extremely well. He was very flexible and did the Tippett operas well. I think that possibly I'm tempted to say he did the best Wozzeck I've done – but then there was John Pritchard's, that was hard to beat. . . . . At the same time I thought the orchestra wasn't at its best with him, especially in the beginning. After we'd had that sort of stardom with Solti, when it was taken away it made us feel a bit down. Colin is so modest and self-effacing – and he included us in his self-effacement. If something went wrong he would sometimes say to the singers, "Oh! I'm terribly sorry. It's our fault". That was rather irritating because it wasn't really our fault. It may have been his. We went through rather a low with him, especially in the early days because we'd had this sort of stardom with Solti and a high profile and this was all taken away.

JT: Do you think the Royal Opera House orchestra takes on the personality of the music director?

HN: I don't know if it takes on his personality. Things have changed. With Kubelik, yes; Solti, yes; with Colin Davis I think the orchestra fought against taking on his personality. Since then we haven't really had a permanent music director. Bernard Haitink is possibly the best conductor in the world, and his performances are absolutely wonderful – with Bernard and a good cast it's really tremendous. But we don't see enough of him to borrow his personality, or to become his well-trained orchestra and that's a great pity. One understands the reason for it, but it's not quite the same as it used to be.

JT: Isn't it like that all over the world?

HN: I'm sure that's so. You could say that conductors get paid too much to travel around. It's a great pity it's gone that way.

JT: You feel things have changed a great deal over the years?

HN: Yes, I do. It is very different now. I think there are several reasons. The point I made earlier – that you have a different orchestra each night – is important, and then the coming and going of conductors is unsettling, too. I feel that the average standard today is much lower than it used to be. It was never brilliant, but we had more good conductors in the old days.

JT: Are there any available now?

HN: Are they available, and can we afford them? There are not many, for certain. In the 1950s and 1960s we were almost the only great opera house in the world that functioned as well as we did. Now there are so many. In those days great conductors and singers would come because it was an honour to sing at Covent Garden, so the money didn't matter. We didn't have money then and we haven't today. But they came because it was a great opera house. Now they can go to so many other great opera houses.

JT: Do you feel that that awareness affected the way you felt about being in the orchestra?

HN: It must have done. The reason for being in that orchestra, and staying, is quite simple. It hasn't been the money or the pleasure of blowing down a brass tube. Why you do the job is because of your love of opera. You're crazy about opera. There is no more complete art form than opera. So, you want to hear it as well done as possible – with great singers and a great conductor. That's what makes you survive in the job. That's all you want: there's nothing else. It's disappointing that most of the time – a high percentage of the time now – you have to go through things which are second best. And that's very irritating. But you survive for the good ones – with Bernard, and one or two others.

JT: Like the Boheme with Carlos Kleiber?

HN: I find Boheme staggering. I think it's the most perfect opera. I don't necessarily mean the best opera, or the best music – but it's perfect! It's the right length, the dramatic build up is right, the parts are right, everything is wonderful – and we know it better than any other opera. The year Kleiber came to do it with us we had just recorded it with Colin Davis. We had finished all the recording sessions when Kleiber appeared. There were 11 rehearsals – and we all sat there enthralled. That was because we really like opera and we really respected him. But that was a one-off. Unfortunately you have to wait several years before you have that experience again. Another great conductor we had recently was Valery Gergiev. He did Eugene Onegin.

JT: When you were a young man would you say that playing for the opera was noticeably different from playing in a symphony orchestra?

HN: Yes, it was entirely different. I'm tempted to say it was a matter of warmth really. When you sit in the pit playing for opera even if you are sitting on the back desk of one of the string sections, you are involved in the drama that's going on up on the stage. You can't avoid it. The atmosphere is charged. You don't get that in the concert hall. You get a good, almost academic performance of a Brahms Symphony, or whatever, and you are slightly concerned that you have played perfectly or that you fitted in. You don't play like that for the opera. You play slightly crazy at times. I think that was Carlos Kleiber's phrase – he said it several times "At this point you must be crazy". And he was absolutely right – you must!

In the case of the brass, my department, some nights you may sit for 10 or 15 minutes not playing a note, but we'll listen, of course, and that tremendous drama is happening up there on stage. Then you come in. By this time you're really bursting and want to do your very best. So it is much more highly charged and much more emotional. And certainly much more interesting.

II. David Theodore

David Theodore's career began in 1969 when he was appointed to the principal oboe chair of the BBC Welsh Orchestra. He was offered this post whilst he was still studying at the Royal Academy of Music. Since then he has been principal oboe of the BBC Symphony, London Philharmonic and Royal Opera Orchestras. After just over four years with the Royal Opera, he returned to the BBC Symphony Orchestra and then in 1990, the London philharmonic orchestra, where he is currently the principal oboe. He also has a busy career as a soloist and chamber musician. He is a professor of the oboe at the Royal Academy of Music.

It is now exactly twenty-five years since I became a professional musician, a period of considerable change in the music profession. Whether these changes have been for better or worse is debatable, but musicians have certainly had to adapt quite rapidly. A major factor behind these changes has been the reduction of state funding for music. Private enterprise has taken over and we find ourselves much more in the market place where rates and conditions are more competitive. Symphony orchestras are by their nature labour intensive and in some ways out of place at present when there is a trend to slim everything down for maximum efficiency. Being a musician has always been considered a precarious occupation and nowadays this is certainly the case: we are all chasing an ever-decreasing amount of work.

I started to learn the oboe as part of a scheme set up by the local education authority in Montgomeryshire (Montgomeryshire has been swallowed up, along with other counties, to become Powys). Looking back, one realises that this was a very enlightened policy enabling children from different backgrounds to have free lessons, from good teachers on instruments loaned by the authority. Until recently, if children showed sufficient musical talent, they were given every encouragement to nurture their ability. It seems that a change has taken place and that, increasingly, only those children whose parents can afford to pay for their children's lessons will be able to have instrumental tuition. This could well result in there being sections of our society from which the musical talent will remain untapped.

The first oboist who made a really big impression on me was Leon Goossens, who was at that time coming to the end of a long and very distinguished career. He had made a number of recordings and they had made a great impression on me; there was a flexibility in his phrasing and sensitivity in his style which made me feel that I wanted to play like that and that the oboe was for me. It is interesting to listen to those recordings again now, and realise how much styles have changed. Instruments and reeds were not as good in Goossens's day so you got used to occasional technical imperfections. His slow, wide vibrato would probably not be acceptable today, but he was the first great oboist I heard and I still feel a thrill whenever I hear his playing.

Whilst I was still studying at the Royal Academy of Music in London I saw the position of principal oboe in the BBC Welsh Orchestra advertised in the Daily Telegraph – the Saturday edition of the Telegraph is where most of the important orchestral vacancies are advertised. Though it was presumptuous of me at the age of twenty, I applied and was offered an audition. I was fortunate. I had prepared all the orchestral excerpts I could find, and must have satisfied the judges that I had what was required: to my great surprise I was offered the job.

My first day with the orchestra, in February 1969, was a most important day in my life. I suddenly realised that the gulf between being a student and a fully-fledged professional was very wide. I still find with my own students that however much I tell them about the finer points of orchestral technique, it is only when they actually start to do the job themselves that they learn what is really required to be a good orchestral musician. There seems to be no substitute for experiencing the reality of playing with other musicians in an orchestra.

At that time there were a substantial number of BBC orchestras; some of them performed the symphonic repertoire, whilst the others played various types of lighter music. The 1960s and 1970s were good times for musicians; the BBC employed more musicians than at present.

As well as their contract orchestras, the BBC also provided a considerable amount of freelance work and chamber music opportunities. For younger players this was a great chance to get started as producers were always on the lookout for new talent in both performers and composers.

Then, in 1966 the BBC created their own Training Orchestras (later the Academy of the BBC). This was a sort of halfway house where students, after leaving music college, could learn the techniques of orchestral playing. It showed great foresight on the part of the BBC, and its eventual demise in the mid-seventies once again left that great gulf between music college and the real world of the professional musician. In 1979 the National Centre for Orchestral Studies was established, funded by the BBC, the Musician's Union and the IBA, and provided with accommodation and academic support by University of London, Goldsmiths' College. This was a very successful and well-organised scheme which unfortunately was obliged to close in 1989 through lack of sufficient funding.

After four years, in 1973, I left the BBC Welsh Orchestra to join the BBC Symphony Orchestra as principal oboe. My predecessor had been Terence McDonagh, whose playing I admired enormously and who probably influenced my style of playing more than anyone else. He had been for many years principal oboe in Beecham's Royal Philharmonic and played in a wind section which set new standards in orchestral playing. They were acclaimed for the fine balance of playing as a well-tuned section and for expressive solos played with great character and distinction.

The early 1970s were heady days for the BBC Symphony Orchestra. William Glock (later Sir William) was then Controller of Music. He took a particular interest in the Symphony orchestra's repertoire, and had appointed Pierre Boulez as Principal Conductor. This proved to be a very enlightened decision. Boulez was to play a major part in changing attitudes to modern music in Britain. His concerts would often consist entirely of rather inaccessible contemporary music. His programming was uncompromising with no sweeteners in what was a heavy intellectual 'diet'. You could either take it or leave it but I do remember that audience figures gradually increased during his time.

Rehearsals with Boulez were always very intensive and detailed. Although many in the orchestra disliked a lot of the music they were obliged to play, everyone felt that with Boulez conducting everything we played was played well. British musicians, in general, dislike over-rehearsing, justifiably so on occasions when an incompetent conductor can really waste time: one never wasted time with Boulez.

After ten years working in the secure environment of the BBC I felt it was time to experience the dangers of a non-contract orchestra. In 1979 I joined the London

Philharmonic Orchestra. At that time Bernard Haitink was the Music Director. This was one of the main reasons why I wanted to join this orchestra. I have always found his musicianship so instinctive; everything he does seems to be right. Having experienced Boulez's marvellously precise and cerebral approach to music, it was interesting to work with Haitink who says very little – his marvellous stick technique somehow always manages to show you just what he wants.

Everyday life in the London Philharmonic proved to be very different from what I had experienced in the BBC Symphony Orchestra. The London Philharmonic is what is called a self-managed orchestra (as are the London Symphony Orchestra, Royal Philharmonic Orchestra and the Philharmonia.) Even though it is seen as a rather uncertain existence, the players in non-contract orchestras seem to thrive on this insecurity. This has always puzzled me; one would expect musicians with a regular contract to be more contented, than those in a less secure situation. Perhaps it is because when you first start to play an instrument there is already a basic insecurity. You are never quite sure whether you will hit the right notes, or if you will please your teacher. Later this uncertainty extends to whether or not you will cope with playing in public. When as musicians we find ourselves in an orchestra in which we enjoy the comforts of a secure position, our inherent insecurity is often at loggerheads with being too comfortable. I think that on the whole, musicians thrive on a certain amount of rough and tumble.

The London Philharmonic is run by a Board of Management made up of musicians from the Orchestra. The Managing Director and administrative staff are employed for the everyday running of the company, but, in theory, policy decisions are made by the Orchestra. On the whole I think the system works well and to some extent the players feel they have control over their own destiny.

It was whilst I was in the London Philharmonic that I had my first introduction to the world of opera. In the summer months, the orchestra moved down to East Sussex to become the resident orchestra for the Glyndebourne Festival Opera. The combination of marvellous music in such a superb setting is quite magnificent. Opera has always seemed to me to be the ideal art form – combining music with drama and visual delights. After I had been in the London Philharmonic for some years the opportunity arose for me to join the Orchestra of the Royal Opera House, Covent Garden. I was delighted and I enjoyed a number of years playing for some wonderful conductors and listening to outstanding world-class singers. I have no doubt that the best music is to be found in the opera house.

The operatic repertoire provides some of the best oboe parts and intensely beautiful solos. Of course the disciplines required for playing opera are in some ways very different from those required when playing on the concert platform. A major difference is that performances of opera are often very much longer. A Wagner opera can last up to five hours so it is essential to pace oneself if one is not to become overtired before one gets to the last act. Because one is often playing for such a long time, one develops a different technique to cope with this problem. In the case of the oboe for instance you learn to play on a type of reed which is not so taxing on the lip without losing the sound quality and flexibility. Obviously standards must remain the same, but somehow one has to achieve the same results with less effort. On the other had there is usually less pressure on the players in an opera orchestra. When one is only part of the overall performance it is possible to hold back a little from time to time. In a symphony concert, which usually only lasts for two hours or so, the demands made on each player, especially the wind principals, is often much more concentrated.

The Royal Opera Orchestra plays for both opera and ballet performances. Musicians can often find playing for the ballet frustrating. Ballet performances can also be long and physically hard work, and even when the music is of the highest standard, one is always aware that one is playing 'second fiddle' to the dancers.

Some of the finest conducting I have experienced has been in the opera house where the skill of a conductor is tested to the limit. There are so many different elements that have to be brought together before work can begin to start on the interpretation. However, on a good night, when everything falls into place, it can be quite a fantastic experience. Some of the great moments that I recall include Verdi's Otello, with Carlos Kleiber; the performances were so highly charged and vital. His conducting technique is remarkably clear and so inspiring that even though he asks for many more rehearsals than most conductors, in fact he needs only a limited amount of his rehearsal time. One knows exactly what he wants and so one just follows him.

Der Rosenkavalier with Bernard Haitink was another highlight. The opera is very long but with his skill in pacing the music there was never a dull moment. Sir Colin Davis is for me, a master of the Mozart operas. He has an instinctive feel for phrasing and chooses tempi that always seem to be just right.

Now, after several years in the opera house with so many experiences to treasure, I have returned to the London Philharmonic Orchestra. At present, half my work is with the LPO and the rest of my time is taken up with freelance work. My freelance work allows me to enjoy a varied musical 'diet'. A good deal of this work is in the commercial field, sadly a diminishing market. American film companies often come to London to record music for their soundtracks. One of the reasons for this is because they think that British musicians can record the music faster. There is also a considerable amount of work for recording the soundtracks for television plays and films. This can be rewarding as the composers are often very skilled. I can't help thinking that if Mozart was alive today he would be writing music for films and TV. I have always felt this need to diversify. It has always seemed to me that the most enthusiastic musicians are those who are able to enjoy a variety of music-making.

It has always been difficult for the symphony orchestras in Britain, and for some time it has been getting even more difficult. Over the past fifteen years, the government has gradually reduced its provision for the arts. This has led the orchestras to rely increasingly on sponsorship. With the continuing recession over the past few years the number of arts organisations seeking financial assistance from sponsors has created a very competitive, even hostile atmosphere.

Recently the Arts Council tried to reduce the number of orchestras working in London. The way this was carried out showed an extraordinary lack of understanding of how the music world works and succeeded only in causing a great deal of distress among the musicians concerned.

However, it is not all doom and gloom. There have been some very worthwhile developments. For example, it is now a major requirement that symphony orchestras should take an active part in music education and create a separate education department within their structure. Sponsors also like to be seen supporting educational projects! Twenty years ago there were schools concerts. I remember them as being very stiff occasions. Nowadays there are some really talented musicians working in the field of education, nurturing an interest in music and showing the children that music really is for them, and not just for boring 'grown-ups'.

I firmly believe that it is vital for a nation to maintain a healthy concern for the arts. Once an arts institution is lost, it will probably have gone for ever.

Musical Performance,
1996, Vol. 1, Part 1, pp. 57–60
Reprints available directly from the publisher
Photocopying permitted by license only

Stravinsky remembered

Basil Tschaikov

Igor Stravinsky. Photo: Richard Avedon. By permission of Sony Classical.

In 1965 Igor Stravinsky made his last appearance in Britain conducting his Firebird Suite, in the 1945 version. The orchestra was the New Philharmonia[1]. Although Stravinsky had conducted in the United Kingdom a number of times, this performance received a public ovation of exceptional intensity, as can be heard and seen on the video archive-recording of the event at the MPRC Listening Studio. The author took part in this performance. He had previously played for Stravinsky in the Philharmonia and Royal Philharmonic Orchestras. Here he remembers his experiences performing under the direction of this legendary composer.

In a lifetime in the world of music, and for many years as an orchestral musician, I had the good fortune to come in contact with a considerable number of remarkable and outstanding men and women. Legendary artists that include the conductors: Sir Thomas Beecham, Bruno Walter, Otto Klemperer, Herbert von Karajan, and Leonard Bernstein; solo instrumentalists of the stature of Thibaud, Heifetz, Menuhin, Tortelier and Rubinstein; and, of course, above all, composers of great talent and originality, international reputation and acclaim. But to meet genius is another experience altogether.

Stravinsky was certainly a genius. To work with him was good fortune, but to have this opportunity three times was indeed to have been smiled on by the gods.

Igor Stravinsky was born in 1882 so that in 1954, when he came to London to conduct a programme on his own works at a Royal Philharmonic Society concert he was already 72 and one might have expected that he would no longer be at his most vigorous. Though he appeared physically quite frail his mind was as agile and incisive as any I have experienced. His clarity of thought and certainty of intention was exciting in itself. He had the ability to make his wishes as a conductor clear, both in words and by his gestures. Contrary to popular belief a good many composers conduct their own music extremely well, and in a few cases also the music of others. Benjamin Britten, Pierre Boulez, Aaron Copland, and Malcolm Arnold immediately come to mind, and though Michael Tippett, William Walton, and Vaughan Williams lacked technical expertise as conductors they brought a special musical insight to performances of their own music.

Many musicians in the past – before the aural complexities that are now part of our everyday experience were dreamt of – often thought that when composers wrote bars of different metric value the result was just 'paper music', and that absolute accuracy was not expected. In 1936 in his book *Chronicle of my Life*, Stravinsky wrote "With regard to the *Sacre*, which I was tackling for the first time, I was particularly anxious in some of the parts (*Glorification of the Elect, Evocation of Ancestors, Dance of Consecration*) to give the bars their true metric value, and to have them played exactly as they were written. I lay stress on this point, which may seem to the reader to be a purely professional detail. But with a few exceptions, such as Monteux and Ansermet, for example, most conductors are inclined to cope with the metric difficulties of these passages in such a cavalier fashion as to distort alike my music and my intentions. This is what happens. Fearing to make a mistake in a sequence of bars of varying values, some conductors do not hesitate to ease their task by treating them as of equal length. By such methods the strong and weak tempi are obviously displaced, and it is left to the musicians

[1] Between 1964 and 1977 the Philharmonia Orchestra was called the New Philharmonia Orchestra.

to perform the onerous task of re-adjusting the accents in the new bars as improvised by the conductors, a task so difficult that even if there is no catastrophe the listener expects one at any moment, and is immersed in an atmosphere of intolerable strain."

Monteux's long association with Stravinsky was celebrated at a concert given by the London Symphony Orchestra at the Royal Albert Hall on the 29th May 1963. On that date, exactly 50 years previously, Monteux had conducted the first performance of *Sacre*. In 1913 the work created a *scandale*; the audience were so inflamed and noisy that Nijinsky had been obliged to stand on a chair at the side of the stage and shout out the numbers to the dancers. On this occasion Stravinsky, who earlier that evening had attended a performance of one of his ballets at Covent Garden, only arrived in time to hear the second half of this work, which even in 1963 was infrequently performed and one that orchestras still found difficult, to witness the tremendous ovation this previously controversial music received. The orchestra were unaware of his presence and it came as a surprise to see the very elderly Pierre Monteux leave the platform to make his way through the audience to greet Stravinsky who was sitting in one of the boxes. The sight of these two veterans of 20th-century music embracing with such affection was very moving and a sight no-one present is likely to forget.

When I recall the rehearsals in 1954 with the Royal Philharmonic Orchestra, it is particularly the rehearsals for *Orpheus*. A feature of much of Stravinsky's music is the use of small note values: sixteenth, thirty-second and sixty-forth notes. Combined with many changes of time signature, varying through 3/4, 2/8, 7/16, etc. these very small note values call for great accuracy of performance. I had already worked with Ernest Ansermet, praised by Stravinsky, when we recorded the original version of *Petrouchka* with the London Philharmonic in 1945, (I was also to take part in the recording of the complete ballet music for *Firebird* when Ansermet conducted the New Philharmonia many years later in the late 1960s). But this had not prepared me for the extreme precision that Stravinsky demanded and achieved. One felt his intelligence was like a razor-sharp blade, stripping away everything that was inessential and dross.

In the interval of the concert he was presented with the Gold Medal of the Royal Philharmonic Society. Perhaps because only that which is true and without blemish was acceptable to him, and pursuing this ideal with his usual concentration of purpose, when he was presented with the medal by Sir Arthur Bliss, he put it between his teeth and gave it an examining bite. Fortunately for the honour of the Society and the composure of Sir Arthur the medal passed this rigorous test and received Stravinsky's approbation.

In the summer of 1963 the Philharmonia was on an extensive tour of South America. Rather unexpectedly, in the middle of the tour, we abandoned our conductors and repertoire to undertake a concert in Rio de Janeiro with Stravinsky and his close associate Robert Craft. The programme consisted of *Fireworks*, *Symphony in C*, and the ballet music for *Baiser de la Fée*, which Stravinsky conducted. In the years since 1954 he had become even more frail, but his mind was as clear and precise as before, and the performance was exact and memorable.

The third and last occasion when Stravinsky enriched my experience was in September 1965. He was now a mere wisp of a man, ill, and it seemed somewhat dejected, or perhaps just tired. He had flown to London from Hamburg to appear at the Royal Festival Hall for the European premiere of his *Variations in Memory of Aldous Huxley*. The other works in the programme were, *Fireworks, The Rite of Spring* and *The Firebird Suite* in the infrequently performed 1945 version. The *Fireworks* and *The Firebird Suite* were the only works he conducted. Again Robert Craft was his associate conductor.

Though he was unwell, during the interval of the rehearsal, as he sat, cosseted by his wife and wrapped in towels and blankets, he was kind enough to inscribe a copy of his *Conversations with Robert Craft*. A copy of that signature, at the head of this tribute, is testimony to the energy that still propelled this remarkable man, now 83, through a creative life spanning over 60 years, during which he had startled, affronted, and delighted generations of audiences.

What I *remember* is that it was a wonderful performance of the *Firebird*. The orchestra was first class; as can happen on very special occasions, when in the presence of someone inspirational, someone for whom everyone has respect, the orchestra rose above itself. Every member of the orchestra took risks: played softer and louder than was safe, extended and contracted rhythms and dynamics, attacked entries with abandon. That is what I *remember*.

Now, thirty years later it is no longer necessary to rely on the ageing memories of elderly musicians or members of the audience who were present on that historic evening. The second half of the programme was televised by the BBC. Robert Craft conducted the *Variations in Memory of Aldous Huxley*, and then Stravinsky conducted the *Firebird Suite*. Recently the Music Performance Research Centre acquired a copy of this wonderful video, on Licence, from the BBC. If you visit the MPRC Listening Studio in the Barbican Library, in the Barbican Centre, you will be able to *see and hear*, in splendid sound, this truly unique performance for yourself.

Musical Performance,
1996, Vol. 1, Part 1, pp. 61–65
Reprints available directly from the publisher
Photocopying permitted by license only

Listening to Music: Alone or in Company

David Coronel

Benjamin Britten stated in his Aspen Lecture of 1964 that every musical experience requires a composer, a performer and a listener. One of the aims of this journal is to include views from the audience as well as from performers and composers.

David Coronel regularly attends concerts and opera performances and also collects recordings. In this article he reflects on the responses he and other music lovers experience in these differing environments.

We are all potential musicians, but some of us are better at it than others. When we listen to a piece of music, of whatever genre, in whatever environment, we all to some extent want to join in. Of course, our natural self-control prevents us from embarrassing ourselves, but when the circumstances permit we will often let rip. Do you sing in the bath, for example? Or conduct whilst listening to a recording? These are (usually) solitary activities, which we only indulge when no-one is listening, but what about dancing to a live band in a ballroom or to records at a discotheque? Or even applauding at the end of a concert? We naturally want to applaud more loudly if we have enjoyed the performance – is this because we have to release a pent-up desire to join in, which is stronger the more involved we have been in the music?

In an ideal world, we would all be virtuosi, capable of picking up a violin and rattling off a Bach Partita at a moment's notice; in reality, most of us have to make do with letting others make music, leaving us to be listeners. Yet not having any ability to sing properly or play an instrument doesn't necessarily make us any less musical. We may dream of standing on the stage of the Royal Opera House, Covent Garden, singing arias to great acclaim, even if we actually sound like a frog with laryngitis. The closest many of us can normally come to achieving such desires is to sit in the audience and allow our imagination to take control. Listening to a recording, even a live relay on the radio or television, is that much less satisfying because we are not physically in the same place as the actual performer; the experience, and the opportunity to dream, is therefore diminished.

We may not realise that the degree to which our subconscious desires are satisfied owes as much to the circumstances in which we hear music as to the music itself. This explains the increasing level of pleasure each of the following musical experiences provides:

listening to a studio recording;
listening to a live recording;
being present at a live performance;
taking part in a live performance.

It is possible to subdivide these categories; for example, in the United Kingdom there is a long-standing tradition of Recorded Music Societies which dates back to the days of pre-electric recording in the early 1920s. Groups of between 10 and 150 people meet regularly to listen to programmes of recorded music introduced by a speaker, and in so doing they introduce two elements of live music-making into their experience. Firstly, the presence of a speaker delivering a script turns the event into something of a live performance; secondly, listening *en masse* removes many of the inadequacies of listening to a recording in one's own home – one has to concentrate on the music being played, without the many distractions of domestic life, and one can directly interact with one's fellow listeners, expressing satisfaction or dissatisfaction with the choice of music, standard of performance and so on, just as one might in the foyer of a concert hall or opera house during the interval or after a concert.

A further subdivision can be made within the concept of listening to a live recording. Playing a recording one may already have heard of a live performance which took place, perhaps, many years ago, *cannot* be as fulfilling as listening to a live relay being broadcast from a concert hall or theatre. As soon as one has heard a recording once, the element of anticipation is missing from subsequent hearings. It is also worth making the point that in these high-technology days, a live recording does not necessarily mean an unedited one, and here are some examples. It is commonly the case that a commercially issued live recording (particularly of opera) is put together from tapes made at a number of different performances, and even sometimes at the rehearsals (acoustics permitting). A recent telecast of a performance of Tchaikovsky's *Eugene Onegin* from Glyndebourne consisted of two acts recorded earlier in the week of transmission, followed by the third act live. I was present at a concert recently from which 'highlights' were broadcast on television the following night. In the concert, *Siegfried's Funeral March* from Wagner's *Götterdämmerung* was followed immediately, without a pause and without applause, by the *Immolation Scene* from the same opera. In the broadcast, filmed applause, including shots of the orchestra standing and the conductor taking a bow, was inserted between the two pieces, and the announcer then spoke his piece about the second extract. In some ways, this third example is the worst, in that the no doubt conscious decision of the musicians to play the two pieces continuously was overturned by those in charge of the transmission. Even if this was done with the musicians' agreement, it was still a form of compromise.

But why should we feel that a recording of a public performance is superior to a studio performance, if it is true that such a recording is just as likely to be a patchwork of separate performances as a studio recording? Here we must call upon the old adage that 'familiarity breeds contempt' – or to put it more mildly, 'frequent repetition breeds boredom'. Music suffers less from this problem than many other art-forms, particularly visual art-forms such as film, after all, it is not uncommon for people to have listened to the same piece of music even hundreds of times, but it is rare for someone to have seen the same film, or perhaps read the same novel, with equivalent frequency.

One could extend our more favourable response to recordings of public performances to explain why it is often felt that older recordings are superior to those made more recently, despite the improvements brought by modern recording techniques. Until forty-five years ago, technology did not permit the over-editing of tapes in an attempt to produce the 'perfect' performance; recordings made before the introduction of tape consist of complete 'takes' with a minimum of interference by the engineers. However clever the technicians have become, any patchwork performance must lose some of its artistic purity. Even if listeners cannot detect the joins, perhaps they may not now always get as much satisfaction from a recording as previously because they are unconsciously reacting to its lack of integrity.

There is often a tendency to compare current practitioners unfavourably with their colleagues of the past, whether they are soldiers, politicians, sportsmen, architects or musicians. In most cases the comparison must be very subjective, because we are unable to provide a precise context within which their achievements are strictly equivalent – for example, who can say for sure whether Napoleon or Julius Caesar was the better military leader? Can one really compare architects of the seventeenth and twentieth centuries when tastes in design and the materials and techniques of building have changed? But in the field of music, we *are* able to make comparisons using the legacy of historical recordings. For example, we can compare a violinist of the early twentieth century with one of the late twentieth century playing the *same* piece of music. And yet, is the comparison fair? Even if we ignore the stylistic changes that have taken place during the past hundred years, and try to concentrate purely on artistic satisfaction, might we not be treating the modern musician too harshly when their recording may suffer far more from the patchwork effect than their predecessor's did? In any case, the very fact that a recording of a performance has been in existence for many years will often make it more acceptable than one which is more recent, simply because of the listener's familiarity with it. It is often the case that the first recording of a work that one purchases affects the way one expects the work to be performed *for the rest of one's life*, even if that recording contains errors or interpretive idiosyncrasies that many may not be able to accept.

It should also be remembered that although there may be some musicians whose abilities are flattered by recording, there are also some for whom recording does no justice. Manipulation of their tone and dynamics by well-intentioned engineers in the recording studio may rob them of their individuality or they may not be temperamentally suited to the rigours of recording sessions – some may feel that they cannot give of their best without the feedback of an audience, whilst others may find it difficult to maintain a consistent level of artistic feeling when compiling a performance from short 'takes'. It can therefore be the case that if one is frequently exposed to the sound of an artist in one's domestic environment, irrespective of the quality of the recording or the equipment, one may get a completely false impression of what that artist sounds like in the concert hall.

It often takes many years for historical changes in style to be accepted by the public, so that a modern recording may well appeal to fewer listeners than one performed in an older and more familiar style. The increasing number of 'period' performances during the past thirty years is a case in point. There are many who find the sound of pre-nineteenth century instruments unattractive, or who miss the 'romantic' style of interpretation of classical or baroque music. Are we in a position to compare a performance of the Beethoven symphonies by Wilhelm Fürtwängler with those made more recently by Roger Norrington, when perhaps most listeners would still regard the former as 'normal' and the latter as 'specialist'? The relative novelty of period style may put off at least as many as it attracts, irrespective of the virtues of the performance as an interpretation of Beethoven's music. Of course, in the future, period style may become accepted as the norm, at which point we may listen to orchestral recordings of the mid-twentieth century with as much curiosity as we currently do to some of the early-twentieth century that have extremes of phrasing and prominent string portamenti.

Stylistic changes can also affect our musical life in a number of ways. Whilst tastes may change relatively quickly, the infrastructure cannot. Many musical venues throughout the world were designed when bigger was better. Nowadays, when smaller seems to be preferred by many, performances can often be robbed of their full impact by the unsuitability of the concert hall. A recent performance of Bach's *Matthäus-Passion* at the Royal Albert Hall in London (capacity 6,500) with combined forces of only 35 players and singers was a perfect example of this. In a different venue it could have worked much better, as it would probably have done if recorded and heard in a domestic environment. What is really worrying about this is that we may become accustomed to a style of musical performance on recordings which we find cannot be reproduced satisfactorily in the concert hall. As a result, attendances may suffer.

A whole new generation of artists has been created who may sound perfectly fine on record, but who are unsuited to many of the popular venues for performance. The success of the record companies' publicity machines in promoting these artists leads to their engagement in halls that are large enough to accommodate the expected demand for tickets, but within which the audience will find that these artists, because of their limitations, can only give a moderate degree of satisfaction. However, some artists may themselves choose to limit their public appearances to places they feel will suit them, thus severely restricting the opportunities for the public to hear them in concert. Either way the audience loses out.

In many respects, the classical music profession is becoming more like the world of popular music, in which much of the material issued on record cannot be performed outside the studio. This problem can also occur with contemporary classical music, although in a different way. The composer Giles Swayne has written that until the first (studio) performance of his 80-minute-long vocal work *CRY*, he did not believe that the work *could* be performed in public, as it would be too difficult for the artists to achieve in one uninterrupted session. Recent performances, such as that at the 1994 BBC Promenade Concert season in London, have proved him wrong.

How will music lovers respond to these contradictory priorities in future? If our concert and opera venues are not suitable, either for the style of performance that we desire to hear or for the type of artists we want to listen to and see perform on stage, and if some composers in future write in such a way that their works can only be recreated bit-by-bit in the studio, the centuries-old tradition of live performance may wither. We would then lose three of the four categories in our list, and we would be left only with the one that is least satisfactory. This is, of course, the nightmare scenario, but we should not be complacent. So long as we allow musical tastes to be moulded primarily by what we can listen to that has been recorded or broadcast, and not by what we actually go out to hear in the concert hall or opera house, the nightmare could become reality.

We invite contributions on this topic, with a view to publication in future issues of Musical Performance.

Musical Performance,
1996, Vol. 1, Part 1, pp. 67–71
Reprints available directly from the publisher
Photocopying permitted by license only

The MCPS National Discography: Britain's Centralised Recordings Information Centre

Malcolm Tibber

Sound recordings have now been in existence for 118 years; the earliest that still survive date back to 1888. As the international heritage of music recordings, commercial and archive, has grown to massive proportions, it has become increasingly difficult to establish manageable cataloguing systems that provide researchers with quick and comprehensive reference to the vast quantities of recordings in existence.

The National Discography was created in Britain in 1986 to establish a computerised database of recordings in the United Kingdom. The author describes the background to the creation of the Discography and discusses its implications.

In the early 1980s the music industry recognised that a centralised recordings information service was required. By 1986 The Mechanical Copyright Protection Society Limited (MCPS) and the National Sound Archive (NSA) came together to form the National Discography. The National Discography is a wholly owned subsidiary of the MCPS. The National Sound Archive as well as many others now use the Discography on a regular basis.

The core of MCPS's activities is the licensing of its members' works for all mechanical reproductions, by record, video, broadcasting, and multi-media producers. Its members comprise music publishers and composers. Since its creation in the early part of this century, MCPS has built up an index of musical works, now computerised. In the mid 1980s, in order to improve the service it was offering to its members, it was decided to create a product profile, giving detailed information on all UK releases.

Its brief was to house detailed information on all recordings in the UK, so it began with currently available recordings with the intention, at that time, of proceeding backwards historically so as to capture data on all items since the founding of the record industry. This changed with the advent of the compact disc. Many releases of value have now been re-issued in this format, thus enabling the Discography to capture a great deal of historic information. It soon became apparent that in order to ensure a high level of data capture, we would need to employ a team of specialists covering all genres of music. The Discography now has probably the largest number of expert discographers anywhere in the world (see the reference to the Repertoire Department on page 70).

The National Discography has four main sections.

The Interested Party Authority File

This contains information about individual artists, groups, and companies, with detailed data relating to each of them. For example, for an artist, this file provides the following information: given and performing name and any performing names or pseudonyms; dates of birth and death; gender; what type of artist – conductor, pianist, oboist, or soprano; the genre performed – classical, folk, jazz or pop; whether the performer is a solo artist or a member of a group, or has links with other performers or groups.

For example, Otto Klemperer is shown as linked with the Philharmonia Orchestra; Norbert Brainin with the Amadeus Quartet; Paul McCartney with the Beatles. In all there are now 127,000 artists on this file.

Through its compilation, the National Discography will help to build the most complete collection of sound recordings, ranging from the compact discs of today through to the wax cylinders of the early 1900s.

The Recordings File

This has detailed information on each unique recording of every work. Thus, each individual recording that Herbert von Karajan made of Beethoven's Fifth Symphony is separately identified and contains the work's title; any alternative titles; International Standard Recording Code (ISRC); date of the recording; the venue where the recording took place; the duration; the publication (P) date and name confirming the copyright owner of the recording; origin and type of recording e.g. studio or public performance, audio or audio-visual; the sound type, mono or stereo, analogue or digital; classifications i.e. classical, folk, jazz etc. As previously mentioned, this file now contains information on recordings going right the way back to the end of the last century. It now contains nearly 1,500,000 entries, including the Music Performance Research Centre's catalogue of archive-recordings.

The Works File

This contains a work's title and alternative titles; translated titles; composers, lyricists, arrangers, editors; the original publisher and the UK copyright owner of the work. The title can be accessed using searchwords (any two words out of the title or a combination of title and composer); classical searchwords, which includes the use of keys and opus numbers as part of the search, in addition to the basic searchword facility; compressed title, where one could search under the entire title or the first word or two; name of interested party, which can be a composer, lyricist, arranger, editor or publisher. Currently there are in excess of 2,000,000 works on this file.

The Product File

This can be accessed in the following ways: by product title; by track title; by catalogue number; by record company; by label; by artist (at both product and track level); by product numbers e.g. bar codes, international numbers, matrix numbers etc.; by a keyword search using part of an artist's name and part of the product title. A single product entry would show all of the above plus a complete track listing including composers and durations. So far over 310,000 products have been listed. Every item in the above files is uniquely identified by a computer-generated number and there are detailed links between each file.

I have previously mentioned the ISRC number, which uniquely identifies a recording and is being progressively used by the record industry on an international basis. The network of international copyright societies has agreed to adopt a similar procedure for musical works using an International Standard Work Code (ISWC). This will allow each work to be identified once and will facilitate a much easier flow of information between societies. As part of this exercise there will also be an international set of data standards, so that we will alleviate the current problems of, for instance, different spellings of a composer's name: for example,

Rachmaninov or Rachmaninoff. It has also been agreed that each territory will take full responsibility of its own repertoire: the German Society looking after German works, the French after French works, etc. Each Society will have access to all the other databases.

The Repertoire Department

The team of expert discographers to which I previously referred are in the Repertoire Department. There are six areas of specialisation: Classical, Popular, Jazz/Blues, Folk/Ethnic, Audio-Visual (dealing with repertoire specifically written for radio and television stations) and Repertoire Support, which comprises the National Discography Helpdesk and which deals with what is called Limited Availability Product – those items produced by small local organisations, such as schools and churches, for their own communities and which are not generally commercially available. Within each of these teams we have experts in even more clearly defined areas of music such as opera, country music, dance, religious music, etc. In total, there are 57 members of staff in the specialist department. Many of these are acknowledged experts in their specialist fields, with editors and critics of established magazines, such as *The Gramophone*, and many who are well-known performers in their own right.

It soon became apparent, very early on in the creation of the database, that all the information acquired for the purpose of licensing would be of great benefit in the music industry at large. It has been the intention to market the database and this has been done in a passive way. We will be promoting it more actively when current negotiations with the British Phonographic Industries (BPI), representing all of the major record companies, come to fruition. These negotiations are intended to create a joint venture marketing company for the National Discography database that will give it the support of both sides of the music business. Even without this in place a substantial number of subscribers are already involved, including recording companies, broadcasters, entertainment industry lawyers and accountants, public gramophone libraries, retailers and other copyright societies.

At present there are three services the National Discography can provide.

On-line access ..... allows a user to access our database from their computer, with instant availability of all the files mentioned above. This is currently accessible via both local and international networks and will soon be made available on the Internet.

Downloading data ..... at regular intervals, fortnightly, monthly, quarterly, etc., and at whatever breadth and depth of information the user desires. For the library community this service is available in the MARC format.

The Helpdesk .... answers telephone and fax queries from all sectors of the music business and from the public at large.

It is anticipated that at some time in the not too distant future the Discography will become available on CD-ROM.

As part of the licensing schemes being operated by the Mechanical Protection Copyright Society, all forms of multi-media will soon be included. It is also a long-term aim to develop the database from its current role, containing data on all releases in the UK, to an international one, when it will house information on all releases in all major territories.

The National Discography is at present involved in discussions with many organisations in the entertainment and cultural fields with a view to extending and making available a large amount of additional useful data. When all these negotiations are completed it is confidently anticipated that the National Discography will be the central database for the music industry worldwide.

Musical Performance,
1996, Vol. 1, Part 1, pp. 73–98
Reprints available directly from the publisher
Photocopying permitted by license only

The Music Performance Research Centre: A Selective Catalogue

Jon Tolansky

The MPRC's holdings consist of over a thousand hours of recordings. These are all **archive-recordings**, both audio and video, that is recordings that have not been made for commercial purposes; they cannot be purchased or borrowed. They are of public performances and conversations with performers, dating from the early 1930s to the present time, which at the time of going to press cover a period from 1933 to 1995. Nearly all these recordings do not exist in other archives. The performances are preserved without any editing. Recordings continue to be added to the library.

The Archive is divided into a number of sections.

Audio Archive-Recordings

Archive-recordings of performances made by the MPRC since 1987 (none of these performances were broadcast)

At March 1995 the MPRC had recorded 112 performances. Some particularly interesting and important examples are:

BEETHOVEN, Ludwig van

Piano Concerto No. 3

Radu Lupu, London Symphony Orchestra: Mstislav Rostropovich

Barbican Centre, 11th July 1993

MPRC 0079

On this rare occasion Radu Lupu and Mstislav Rostropovich performed together. The entire concert was recorded by the MPRC (on tape MPRC 0079). The other major work was the world première of the Symphony No. 4 by Vyacheslav ARTYOMOV, entitled 'The Morning Star Arises'. The concert opened with Beethoven's Coriolan Overture.

BERLIOZ, Hector

The Trojans

Jane Henschel, Vladimir Bogachov, Carlos Alvarez, Gwynne Howell, Markella Hatziano, Maria Popescu, Robert Lloyd, London Symphony Chorus, London Symphony Orchestra: Sir Colin Davis

Barbican Centre, 12th December 1993

MPRC 0086, and 0087

This is a recording of a performance of 'The Trojans' that the London Symphony Orchestra mounted in a concert performance, with very large forces: an orchestra of more than 150 players, and a chorus of over 400. On this occasion Part One was played at an afternoon performance and Part Two in the evening. This performance was a rare event; 'The Trojans' is infrequently programmed on account of the large forces required.

JANACEK, Leos

String Quartet No. 1 (Kreutzer)

Brindisi Quartet

Purcell Room, South Bank Centre, London, 31st March 1994

MPRC 0089

This performance was given in the Park Lane Group Young Artists series featuring outstanding young musicians playing classical and contemporary works. The entire concert was recorded by the MPRC (on tape number MPRC 0089), the remaining items being the 3rd String Quartet No 3 of Bela BARTOK, the String Quartet No 1 by Gabriel JACKSON, entitled 'From Schipol to Shannon', and the Concertino for Oboe and String Quartet by David MATTHEWS, with Melinda Maxwell (Oboe).

MAHLER, Gustav

Symphony No. 2

Yvonne Kenny, Yard van Nes, London Philharmonic Choir and London Philharmonic Orchestra: Klaus Tennstedt

Royal Festival Hall, 18th February 1989 and 20th February 1989 – two performances

MPRC 0026, and 0027

Klaus Tennstedt conducted two performances of Mahler's 2nd Symphony. There are some slight but significant differences in tempi and phrasing between the two performances; more striking are the considerable differences between both public performances and the same conductor and orchestra's commercial recording.

MASSENET, Jules

Manon

Leontina Vaduva, David Rendell, Francois le Roux, Royal Opera Chorus and Orchestra: Michel Plasson

Royal Opera House, Covent Garden, 29th November 1988.

MPRC 0021

This was the notable British debut of the Roumanian soprano Leontina Vaduva. At the time of writing she has not made a commercial recording of this role.

MAXWELL DAVIES, Peter

Trumpet Concerto

John Wallace, Philharmonia Orchestra: Giuseppe Sinopoli

Royal Festival Hall, London, 9th October 1988

MPRC 0018

This was the world première of Maxwell Davies's Trumpet Concerto. Also on the programme were the Overture In the South by ELGAR, and Symphony No. 1 by MAHLER. Both these items were also recorded on tape number MPRC 0018.

MOZART, Wolfgang Amadeus

Piano Concerto No. 25, K503, in C

Richard Goode, English Chamber Orchestra: Sir Colin Davis

AND

Serenade for 13 Wind Instruments, in B flat, K 361/370a

English Chamber Orchestra: Sir Colin Davis

Barbican Centre, 5th October 1993

MPRC 0083

This was a rare occasion; two of today's most distinguished interpreters of Mozart's music, Sir Colin Davis and Richard Goode, performed together. The concert opened with the Overture to MOZART's opera Cosi Fan Tutte.

PROKOFIEV, Serge

Romeo and Juliet – a selection from the ballet music, made by Mstislav Rostropovich

Paul Jesson (narrator), London Symphony Orchestra: Mstislav Rostropovich

Barbican Centre, 26th November 1991

MPRC 0062

Mstislav Rostropovich was the artistic director of a Prokofiev Festival held in 1991. For this concert, he created three suites from the complete ballet music. Between each movement a narrator spoke selected extracts from Shakespeare's play.

SAINT-SAËNS, Camille

Samson and Delilah

Placido Domingo, Olga Borodina, Royal Opera Chorus and Orchestra: Mark Ermler

Royal Opera House, Covent Garden, 18th June 1992

MPRC 0071

The Royal Opera considered this a particularly important performance with the Kirov Opera Soprano, Olga Borodina, singing Delilah alongside Placido Domingo's Samson.

SCHOENBERG, Arnold

Gurrelieder

Rita Hunter, John Mitchinson, Christine Cairns, Ian Caley, Brian Bannatyne-Scott, Franz Mazura, CBSO Chorus, Philharmonia Chorus, City of Birmingham Symphony Orchestra (augmented): Sir Simon Rattle

Symphony Hall, Birmingham, 24th September 1994

MPRC 0094

This recording was made at the first performance of 'Gurrelieder' to be heard in Birmingham. Sir Simon Rattle conducted an orchestra of over 160 musicians (Figure 1). He has not made a commercial recording of this work.

Figure 1 Sir Simon Rattle conducting the City of Birmingham Symphony Orchestra.

STOCKHAUSEN, Karlheinz

Momente

Angela Tunstall, Birmingham Contemporary Music Group: Jonty Solomon

Adrian Boult Hall, Birmingham, 13th November 1994

MPRC 0097

This was a rare performance of Stockhausen's large scale work involving groups of musicians performing and also acting in many different areas in the hall.

STRAUSS, Richard

Elektra

Eva Marton, Nadine Secunde, Marjana Lipovsek, Robert Hale: the Royal Opera Chorus and Orchestra: Sir Georg Solti

Royal Opera House, Covent Garden, 23rd March 1990

MPRC 0044

This is the only recording of Eva Marton and Sir Georg Solti (Figure 2) performing together in this opera. They have both made commercial recordings of the work with other artists.

Figure 2 Sir Georg Solti – the conductor of Richard Strauss's 'Elektra' at the Royal Opera House in 1990. By permission of the Decca Record Company.

TIPPETT, Sir Michael

The Vision of St Augustine

David Wilson Johnson, Elaine Pearce, London Sinfonietta, London Sinfonietta Chorus: Elgar Howarth

Barbican Centre, 17th February 1995

MPRC 0101

This performance was part of a long concert, one of several in a festival called "Visions of Paradise" that marked the 90th birthday of Sir Michael Tippett. Also taking part was the Grimethorpe Colliery Band conducted by Elgar Howarth. The entire concert was recorded by the MPRC (on tape number MPRC 0101). The other works were the Salford Toccata by Sir Harrison BIRTWISTLE, Double Entendre by Charles SANSON, and Festal Brass with Blues by TIPPETT, all performed by the Grimethorpe Colliery Band, and the Opening Music to King Priam by TIPPETT, arranged by Elgar HOWARTH, performed by the combined forces of the London Sinfonietta, London Sinfonietta Chorus and Grimethorpe Colliery Band.

TSCHAIKOVSKY, Peter Ilytch

Eugene Onegin

Galina Gorchakova, Sergei Leiferkus, Louise Winter, Gegam Grigorian, Nicolai Ghiaurov: Royal Opera Chorus and Orchestra: Valery Gergiev

Royal Opera House, Covent Garden, 22nd July 1993

MPRC 0080

This performance marked the debut at the Royal Opera House of Valery Gergiev, music director of the Kirov Opera. The two principal roles were taken by Kirov Opera artists.

Four months later, the MPRC recorded, 'off-air', a broadcast of a subsequent performance from the Royal Opera House with a different cast – Dimitri Hvorostovsky and Catherine Malfitano, and conducted by Mark Ermler, with much the same orchestral personnel (MPRC BCT 96). These two recordings give the listener the opportunity to hear the extent to which two performances of the same production can differ.

"Off-air" recordings of broadcast performances dating from 1933 to 1987, donated to the MPRC (to the best of our knowledge none of these exist in any other archive)

At March 1995, the MPRC had placed in its archive 170 performances recorded 'off-air' from broadcasts. All the recordings had been received as donations, including many historically significant performances such as:

BEETHOVEN, Ludwig van

Piano Sonata No. 21 in C major, Opus 53 (the Waldstein)

Rudolf Serkin

AND

SCHUBERT, Franz

Piano Sonata No. 20 in A major, D 959

Usher Hall, Edinburgh, 30th August 1964

MPRC BCT 107

This recital was given during the Edinburgh Festival of 1964. Rudolf Serkin made a commercial studio recording of the Schubert Sonata the same year, and those who are able to compare this with the public performance will find some notable differences.

BERG, Alban

Wozzeck

Jess Walters, Cristel Goltz, Royal Opera Chorus and Orchestra: Erich Kleiber

Royal Opera House, Covent Garden 25th May 1953

MPRC BCT 14

This is one of a series of performances of 'Wozzeck' conducted by Erich Kleiber at Covent Garden. It was the first British stage production of this opera, for which Kleiber had 18 orchestral rehearsals. Erich Kleiber gave the world première of 'Wozzeck' and during his lifetime was widely regarded as the work's most authentic exponent. He never made a commercial recording of the opera.

BERLIOZ, Hector

Grande Messe des Morts

Renee Soames, Luton Choral Society, BBC Chorus (augmented), BBC Symphony Orchestra (augmented): Sir Thomas Beecham

Royal Albert Hall, 10th December 1947

MPRC BCT 6

This performance was notable for the unusually large forces present. On this occasion Sir Thomas Beecham demanded that Berlioz's original intentions be followed as faithfully as possible. The orchestra numbered 172 players, including 19 percussionists, and the chorus numbered over 500.

BOULEZ, Pierre

Le Soleil des Eaux

Josephine Nemdick, Louis de Voss, Barry McDaniel, BBC Chorus, BBC Symphony Orchestra: Pierre Boulez

Royal Festival Hall, London, 4th March 1964

MPRC BCT 128

This performance took place during the concert that marked the London conducting debut of Pierre Boulez.

BRAHMS, Johannes

Clarinet Quintet in E minor

Thea King, Yehudi Menuhin, Robert Masters, Walter Gerhard, Maurice Gendron

Assembly Rooms, Bath, 1964 (precise date unavailable)

MPRC BCT 106

This is a very rare recorded example of Lord Menuhin participating in a chamber music recital, together with several very distinguished soloists.

BRITTEN, Lord Benjamin

War Requiem

Heather Harper, Peter Pears, Dietrich Fischer-Dieskau, Melos Ensemble, Choruses, City of Birmingham Symphony Orchestra: Meredith Davies and Benjamin Britten

Coventry Cathedral, 30th May 1962

MPRC BCT 68

This was the world première of Britten's 'War Requiem'.

DEBUSSY, Claude

Le Martyre de Saint-Sebastien: Orchestral fragments

Philharmonia Orchestra: Guido Cantelli

Usher Hall, Edinburgh, 9th September 1954

AND

SCHUMANN, Robert

Symphony No. 4

Philharmonia Orchestra: Guido Cantelli

Usher Hall, Edinburgh, 9th September 1954

MPRC BCT 114

Both the above works were recorded at the same concert. This is the only known recording of a public performance by Guido Cantelli with the Philharmonia Orchestra. These performances differ from the commercial recordings Cantelli made of these works with this orchestra.

DELIUS, Frederick

A Village Romeo and Juliet

Rene Soames, Lorely Dyer, and other soloists, Chorus and Royal Philharmonic Orchestra: Sir Thomas Beecham

BBC Studio, 16th April 1948

MPRC BCT 12

In 1948 when this 'off-air' recording was made, the broadcast studio performance was very similar to a public performance in that it was continuous and not edited. Within a few weeks the same artists (except for two of the soloists) made a commercial studio recording of the opera. Those who are able to compare the two performances will find notable differences, most noticeable in 'The Walk to the Paradise Garden': the broadcast performance is played far more slowly, and with considerably more rubato and dynamic contrast than the commercial studio recording.

DONIZETTI, Gaetano

Lucia di Lammermoor

Dame Joan Sutherland, Joao Gibin, Royal Opera Chorus and Orchestra: Tulio Serafin

Royal Opera House, Covent Garden, 26th Feburary 1959

MPRC BCT 52

This was the occasion of Joan Sutherland's debut in this role. She created a sensation and became world famous overnight.

LISZT, Franz

Sonata in B Minor

Sviatoslav Richter

Royal Festival Hall, 15th June 1966

MPRC BCT 111

This was one of Sviatoslav Richter's rare public appearances, performing a work of which he has not made a commercial recording. The other works in the recital, all recorded on tape number MPRC BCT 111, were the Prelude Chorale and Fugue by Cesar FRANCK and the Sonata in B, D 575, by Franz SCHUBERT.

Figure 3 Kathleen Ferrier – the soloist in Mahler's Third Symphony with the BBC Symphony Orchestra conducted by Sir Adrian Boult in 1947. By permission of the Decca Record Company.

MAHLER, Gustav

Symphony No. 3 in D minor

Kathleen Ferrier, Chorus, BBC Symphony Orchestra: Sir Adrian Boult

BBC Studio, 29th November 1947

MPRC BCT 5

This was another of those continuous unedited studio performances, like that of Delius's 'Village Romeo and Juliet' (see above MPRC BCT 12). It was part of a series of broadcast performances of Mahler's Symphonies during 1947 and 1948. At that time these symphonies were rarely performed in Britain. This is the only known recording of Kathleen Ferrier (Figure 3) singing in Mahler's Third Symphony, and it is also the only known recording of Sir Adrian Boult conducting this work.

The following public performances in this series of Mahler symphonies were also broadcast, and 'off-air' recordings are housed in the MPRC archive:

Symphony No. 1

London Philharmonic Orchestra: Bruno Walter

Royal Albert Hall, 6th November 1947

MPRC BCT 3

Symphony No. 5

BBC Symphony Orchestra: Sir Adrian Boult

BBC Studio, 20th December 1947

MPRC BCT 7

Symphony No. 7

BBC Symphony Orchestra: Sir Adrian Boult

BBC Studio, 23rd January 1948

MPRC BCT 10

Symphony No. 8

Soloists and Choruses and BBC Symphony Orchestra: Sir Adrian Boult

Royal Albert Hall, 6th February 1948

MPRC BCT 11

MOUSSORGSKY, Modest

Pictures at an Exhibition (Orchestrated by Ravel)

New Philharmonia Orchestra: Riccardo Muti

Fairfield Hall, Croydon, 2nd December 1972

MPRC BCT 40

This was the concert at which Riccardo Muti made his British debut. Shortly afterwards he was appointed the New Philharmonia Orchestra's Principal Conductor, a post he held with considerable influence until 1983. (Between 1964 and 1977 The Philharmonia Orchestra was known as the New Philharmonia Orchestra, following the Philharmonia's suspension by its owner, Walter Legge. It regained its original title in 1977.)

MOUSSORGSKY, Modest

Boris Godunov

Boris Christoff, Royal Opera Chorus and Orchestra: Rafael Kubelik

Royal Opera House, Covent Garden, 6th November 1958

MPRC BCT 20

This is the only known recording of Boris Christoff singing the role of Boris Godunov in an edition of Moussorgsky's original version. He nearly always performed the version arranged by Rimsky-Korsakov.

STRAUSS, Richard

Don Juan

Till Eulenspiegel

Philharmonia Orchestra: Otto Klemperer

Royal Festival Hall, 5th April 1958

MPRC BCT 18

These performances were given approximately 18 months before the same artists made commercial studio recordings of the same music. Those who are able to compare these recordings will find significant differences: in both the public performances there are considerably greater extremes of tempi and dynamics, and some spontaneous changes of tempo that are absent on the studio recording.

STRAUSS, Richard

Der Rosenkavalier

Elisabeth Schwarzkopf, Sena Jurinac, Hanny Steffek, Kurt Bohme, Royal Opera Chorus and Orchestra: Georg Solti

Royal Opera House, Covent Garden, 1959 (precise date unavailable)

MPRC BCT 22

This performance took place during the production that marked Georg Solti's debut at the Royal Opera House, Covent Garden.

Figure 4 Placido Domingo as Otello and Margaret Price as Desdemona in the Royal Opera's production of Verdi's 'Otello' conducted by Carlos Kleiber in 1980. Photography by Clive Barda. By permission of Clive Barda.

VERDI, Giuseppe

Otello

Placido Domingo, Silvano Carroli, Margaret Price, Royal Opera Chorus and Orchestra: Carlos Kleiber

Royal Opera House, Covent Garden, 19th February 1980

MPRC BCT 45

This was an important event. It was the first time Carlos Kleiber conducted 'Otello' at Covent Garden (Figure 4), and his presence created a very powerful impression on performers, audiences and critics. He has not made a commercial recording of the opera.

WAGNER, Richard

Tannhauser: Overture and Venusberg Music

BBC Symphony Orchestra: Arturo Toscanini

Queen's Hall, London, 16th June 1937

MPRC BCT 116

This performance was given during a concert of music by Wagner. It was part of the 1937 London Music Festival, organised by the BBC. The entire concert is housed in the MPRC archive on tape number MPRC BCT 116. The other items were the Faust Overture, Dawn and Siegfried's Rhine Journey from Götterdämmerung, Forest Murmurs from Siegfried, the Preludes to Act 1 and Act 3 of Lohengrin, the Siegfried Idyll, and the Ride of the Valkyries from Die Walkure.

The event was one of several historic concerts given by Toscanini and the BBC Symphony Orchestra, another of which is preserved in the MPRC archive: it is a performance of BEETHOVEN's Symphony No. 9 with soloists Isobel Baillie, Margaret Balfour, Parry Jones and Harold Williams, and the BBC Chorus and BBC Choral Society. This was given on the 3rd of November 1937 at the Queen's Hall, London, and is preserved on tape number MPRC BCT 129.

'Off-air' recordings of broadcast performances taken down by the MPRC since 1987

Since 1987, the MPRC has recorded some performances 'off-air' from broadcasts. Amongst them are these historically important items:

MAHLER, Gustav

Symphony No. 2, The Resurrection

Lynne Dawson, Jean Rigby, massed choruses, Bournemouth Symphony Orchestra: Andrew Litton

Winter Gardens, Bournemouth, 29th May 1993

MPRC BCT 75

This performance was given during the centenary celebrations of the Bournemouth Symphony Orchestra. Its quality was considered by many to represent an important landmark in the development of this orchestra's reputation.

TIPPETT, Sir Michael

A Child of Our Time

Deboral Riedel, Florence Quivar, Laurence Dale, John Tomlinson, London Symphony Chorus, London Symphony Orchestra: Sir Colin Davis

Barbican Centre, London, 5th February 1995

MPRC BCT 154

This was the opening concert in the "Visions of Paradise" Festival celebrating the 90th birthday of Sir Michael Tippett (see notes to MPRC 0101). The composer was present at the performance, which was highly acclaimed by the audience and critics.

Video Archive-Recordings

Performances recorded by the BBC from television relays, and licensed by the BBC to the MPRC (these performances are not commercially available)

BACH, Johann Sebastian

Toccata and Fugue in D Minor (transcribed by Leopold Stokowski)

BAX, Sir Arnold

Tintagel

ENESCU, Georges

Roumanian Rhapsody No 1

PURCELL, Henry

Dido and Aeneas – Dido's Lament (transcribed by Leopold Stokowski)

BBC Symphony Orchestra: Leopold Stokowski

BBC Studio, 7th of March 1954

MPRC VID 2

This was a studio concert in the series "The Conductor Speaks". Leopold Stokowski introduced and discussed all the items.

BEETHOVEN, Ludwig van

Piano Concerto No 4

Artur Rubinstein, London Philharmonic Orchestra: Antal Dorati

Royal Festival Hall, 7th January 1968

MPRC VID 7

This was part of Rubinstein's first televised concert in Britain in which he performed the last three Beethoven piano concertos. The performance was preceded by an interview, in which he spoke with Richard Baker

MOUSSORGSKY, Modest

Boris Godunov (arranged Rimsky-Korsakov) – The Death of Boris

VERDI, Giuseppe

Don Carlos – Ella giammai m'amo

Boris Christoff, Philharmonia Orchestra: Marcus Dods

BBC Studio, 30th October 1962

MPRC VID 3

This was a profile of Boris Christoff, in which he talked with John Freeman and sang staged extracts from two of his most famous roles: King Philip the 2nd and Boris Godunov

RAVEL, Maurice

La Valse

London Symphony Orchestra: Claudio Abbado

Barbican Centre, 3rd of March 1982

MPRC VID 10

This was the concluding work in the concert marking the official opening of the Barbican Centre Arts Complex.

STRAVINSKY, Igor

The Firebird – 1945 Suite from the ballet

New Philharmonia Orchestra: Igor Stravinsky

Royal Festival Hall, 14th September 1965

MPRC VID 5

This performance was the concluding item in a concert that was Stravinsky's last appearance in Britain. It was an historic event that is recalled in this journal by one of the artists taking part, in the article entitled 'Stravinsky Remembered' (page 57).

VERDI, Giuseppe

Requiem Mass

Ilva Ligabue, Grace Bumbry, Sandor Konya, Raffaele Arie, Philharmonia Chorus, Philharmonia Orchestra: Carlo Maria Giulini

Royal Festival Hall, 26th April 1964

MPRC VID 4

This was a performance of the Verdi Requiem that was especially highly acclaimed at the time by audiences and critics. It was also the British debut of mezzo soprano Grace Bumbry. In the interval Carlo Maria Giulini talked with David Attenborough.

Interviews with conductors, singers and instrumentalists

Conductors

CLAUDIO ABBADO

Music Director of the Berlin Philharmonic Orchestra. Previous Music Director posts include the London Symphony Orchestra, La Scala Milan, the Vienna Philharmonic Orchestra, and the Vienna State Opera. Co-founder of the European Community Youth Orchestra and Gustav Mahler Jugend Orchester.

MPRC INT 14

SIR COLIN DAVIS

Principal Conductor of the London Symphony Orchestra. Previous posts include Sadlers Wells Opera, BBC Symphony Orchestra, Royal Opera House Covent Garden and Bavarian Radio Orchestra.

MPRC INT 8

SIR EDWARD DOWNES

Associate Music Director of the Royal Opera House, Covent Garden. Previous Music Director posts include the Australian Opera and BBC Philharmonic Orchestra.

MPRC INT 21

MARK ELDER

Former Music Director of the English National Opera, also Rochester Philharmonic Orchestra.

MPRC INT 22

JAMES JUDD

Music Director of the Florida Philharmonic Orchestra

MPRC INT 24

JOHN LANCHBERY

Former Music Director of the Royal Ballet and Australian National Ballet

MPRC INT 25

LORIN MAAZEL

Music Director of the Pittsburg Symphony Orchestra and Bavarian Radio Orchestra. Former Music Directorships include the Berlin RIAS Orchestra, Cleveland Orchestra, Deutsche Oper am Rhein.

MPRC INT 18

SIR CHARLES MACKERRAS

Principal Guest Conductor of the Royal Philharmonic Orchestra. Former Music Director of the English National Opera and Welsh National Opera.

MPRC INT 1

SIR NEVILLE MARRINER

Founder and Music Director of the Academy of St Martin in the Fields. Formerly Principal Second Violin in the London Symphony Orchestra.

MPRC INT 3

MICHEL PLASSON

Music Director of the Orchestre de la Capitole Toulouse, and of the Toulouse Opera.

MPRC INT 12

SIR SIMON RATTLE

Music Director of the City of Birmingham Symphony Orchestra.

MPRC INT 13

Singers

THOMAS ALLEN

Baritone, opera and lieder. Opera roles include Billy Budd (Billy Budd – Britten), Don Giovanni (Don Giovanni – Mozart), Eisenstein (Die Fledermaus – J Strauss), Onegin (Eugene Onegin – Tschaikovsky), Lescaut (Manon Lescaut – Puccini), Pelleas (Pelleas et Melisande – Debussy). Lieder includes works by Beethoven, Schubert and Schumann.

MPRC INT 5

COLETTE ALLIOT-LUGAZ

Soprano, opera and lieder. Opera roles include L'Enfant (L'Enfant et les Sortileges – Ravel). Lazuli (L'Etoile – Chabrier), Melisande (Pelléas et Melisande – Debussy). Lieder includes works by Debussy and Ravel.

MPRC INT 6

LANDO BARTOLINI

Tenor. Roles include Calaf (Turandot – Puccini), Duke of Mantua (Rigoletto – Verdi), Alfredo (La Traviata – Verdi)

MPRC INT 20

JENNY DRIVALA

Soprano, opera and lieder. Opera roles include Fiordiligi (Cosi fan Tutte – Mozart), Melisande (Pelléas et Melisande – Debussy), Thais (Thais – Massenet), Violetta (La Traviata – Verdi). Lieder includes works by Donizetti, Saint-Saens, Richard Strauss and Weill.

MPRC INT 19

YVONNE KENNY

Soprano, opera and concert. Opera roles include Semele (Semele – Handel), Sophie (Der Rosenkavalier – R Strauss). Concert repertoire includes Mahler's 2nd and 4th Symphonies.

MPRC INT 4

ROBERT LLOYD

Bass baritone, opera. Opera roles include Arkel (Pelléas et Melisande – Debussy), Boris Godunov (Boris Godunov – Moussorgsky), Fafner (Das Rheingold – Wagner), Gurnemanz (Parsifal – Wagner), Telramund (Lohengrin – Wagner).

MPRC INT 11

CAROL NEBLETT

Soprano, opera and concert. Opera roles include Marie/Marietta (Die Tote Stadt – Korngold), Minnie (La Fanciulla del West – Puccini), Musetta (La Boheme – Puccini), Tosca (Tosca – Puccini), Vitellia (la Clemenza di Tito – Mozart). Concert repertoire includes Mahler's 2nd Symphony and Berlioz's Damnation of Faust (Marguerite).

MPRC INT 2

JONATHAN SUMMERS

Baritone, opera. Roles include Balstrode (Peter Grimes – Britten), The High Priest of Dagon (Samson and Delilah – Saint-Saens), Rigoletto (Rigoletto – Verdi), Schaunard (La Boheme – Puccini).

MPRC INT 16

DAME JOAN SUTHERLAND

Soprano, opera. Roles include Angelica (Suor Angelica – Puccini), Esclarmonde (Esclarmonde – Massenet), Lucia (Lucia di Lammermoor – Donizetti), Marguerite (Faust – Gounod), Norma (Norma – Bellini), The Queen of the Night (The Magic Flute – Mozart), Violetta (La Traviata – Verdi).

MPRC INT 17

CAROL VANESS

Soprano, opera. Roles include Leonore (Fidelio – Beethoven), Donna Elvira (The Marriage of Figaro – Mozart), Tosca (Tosca – Puccini), Vitellia (La Clemenza di Tito – Mozart).

MPRC INT 9

Instrumentalists

KURT-HANS GOEDICKE

Timpanist. Principal in the London Symphony Orchestra, since 1964

MPRC INT 31

HUGH MAGUIRE

Violinist. Leader: the London Symphony Orchestra, 1956–1962; BBC Symphony Orchestra Orchestra, 1962–1967; Royal Opera Orchestra, 1984–1993; he also played in the London Philharmonic and Philharmonia Orchestras between 1946–1956

MPRC INT 27

DOUGLAS MILNE

Percussionist. Played in the Philharmonia Orchestra, 1953–1963; Principal, City of Birmingham Symphony Orchestra, 1963–1971 and 1974–1986; and Royal Opera Orchestra 1971–1974)

MPRC INT 38

GARETH MORRIS

Flautist. Principal in the Philharmonia Orchestra, 1948–1971. Chairman of the New Philharmonia Orchestra, 1966–1971. Also a distinguished solo instrumentalist.

MPRC INT 10

DENNIS SCARD

Played the horn in various symphony orchestras in Britain, 1967–1981. General Secretary of the Musicians Union of Great Britain, 1991–

MPRC INT 30

BASIL TSCHAIKOV

Clarinettist. Member of the London Philharmonic Orchestra, 1943–1947; Royal Philharmonic Orchestra, 1947–1955; Philharmonia Orchestra, 1955–1979. Chairman of the New Philharmonia and Philharmonia Orchestra, 1974–1979. Founder and Director of the National Centre for Orchestral Studies,1979–1990. Co-founder and Chairman of the Music Performance Research Centre (1987–).

MPRC INT 39

RICHARD WALTON

Principal trumpet in the London Philharmonic Orchestra, 1932–1940; Royal Philharmonic Orchestra, 1947–1955; Philharmonia Orchestra, 1955–1960; London Philharmonic Orchestra, 1960–1963; BBC Symphony Orchestra, 1963–1978.

MPRC INT 7

The MPRC Oral History of Musicians in Britain

These are in-depth interviews examining the lives and backgrounds of musicians who have performed in Britain

GWYDION BROOKE

Bassoonist. Member of the London Philharmonic Orchestra, 1932 to 1940; Principal in the Royal Philharmonic Orchestra, 1947 to 1959, and Philharmonia Orchestra, 1959 to 1980.

MPRC OH 1

MARTIN GATT

Bassoonist. Principal in the London Symphony Orchestra, 1976 – present.

MPRC OH 7

PHILIP JONES

Principal trumpet in the Royal Philharmonic Orchestra, 1956 to 1960, and Philharmonia Orchestra, 1960 to 1965. Founder of Philip Jones Brass Ensemble. Principal of Trinity College of Music, 1988 to 1994.

MPRC OH 6

JOHN LUDLOW

Violinist. Leader, London Concert Orchestra, also played in the Royal Philharmonic Orchestra, 1950s and 1960s.

MPRC OH 8

GARETH MORRIS

Flautist. Principal in the Philharmonia Orchestra, 1948 to 1971. Chairman of the New Philharmonia Orchestra, 1966 to 1971. Also a distinguished solo instrumentalist.

MPRC OH 5

ANTHONY PINI

'cellist. Performed in orchestras from 1918 to 1975. Principal in the London Philharmonic Orchestra, 1930s, Royal Philharmonic Orchestra, 1940s and 1950s, and Royal Opera Orchestra, 1960s and 1970s. Also a distinguished soloist.

MPRC OH 2

RICHARD RAMSAY-HILL

Violinist. Played in cinemas during the 'silent' cinema days, in restaurants, for summer seasons – finally for some years with Max Jaffa – and in theatres, from the 1920's until the 1970's.

MPRC OH 3

EVELYN ROTHWELL

Oboist. Member of the Scottish Orchestra, 1930s. Glyndebourne Opera, 1930s. Also a distinguished soloist. Married Sir John Barbirolli.

MPRC OH 11

WILLIAM WALLER

Played the horn in a wide range of venues from 1914 onwards. At the time of this interview he had just celebrated his 100th birthday. The later part of his career was spent in the Royal Liverpool Philharmonic Orchestra.

MPRC OH 4

MARIE WILSON

Violinist. Member of the Queen's Hall Orchestra, 1920s; BBC Symphony Orchestra, 1930s, (Leader, section C); Philharmonia Orchestra, 1950s; and London Philharmonic Orchestra, 1960s, '70s, and '80s.

MPRC OH 10

MPRC Special Collections

These are collections of 'off-air' recordings of performances of certain artists, giving an overview of their work

The MPRC/Sir Arthur Bliss Collection consists of performances of the music of Bliss recorded between 1956 and 1983.

The MPRC/City of Birmingham Symphony Orchestra consists of performances given by the City of Birmingham Symphony Orchestra between 1957 and 1995.[1]

The MPRC/Dame Kiri Te Kanawa Collection consists of performances given by Dame Kiri between 1973 and 1990.[1]

The MPRC/Lorin Maazel Collection consists of performances given by Lorin Maazel between 1960 and 1981.

The MPRC/BBC Salon Orchestra Collection consists of performances given by the BBC Salon Orchestra in 1942 and 1943.

The MPRC/Lew Stone Collection consists of performances given by Lew Stone and his Band between 1934 and 1967.

MPRC Documentaries

These are historical documentaries made by the MPRC, with the inclusion of many recorded conversations with performers

SIR THOMAS BEECHAM

Sir Thomas Beecham remembered by Basil Tschaikov and many of his colleagues, who all played with Sir Thomas for many years

MPRC DOC 2

[1] Including MPRC on-site recordings of public performances.

THE CITY OF BIRMINGHAM SYMPHONY ORCHESTRA

A portrait of the CBSO's life from 1957 to 1991, with extracts from the MPRC/CBSO Collection of performances, and spoken contributions from many CBSO artists

MPRC DOC 3

THE PHILHARMONIA TRADITION

The life and history of the Philharmonia Orchestra, from its foundation in 1945 to its 50th anniversary in 1995, in the words of its past and present members and several conductors.

MPRC DOC 1

Musical Performance
1996, Vol. 1, Part 1, pp. 99–100
Reprints available directly from the publisher
Photocopying permitted by license only

Notes on Contributors

David Coronel is Registrar of the Federation of Recorded Music Societies and Secretary of the Orpington Recorded Music Society. As well as being an ardent record collector he sings in a number of choirs, one of which he conducts, and regularly attends concert and opera performances.

Robert Lloyd studied at Oxford University as an historian. He did not start his distinguished singing career (he has a considerable discography of over 70 audio and video recordings) until he was 28.

In 1972 he was appointed principal bass at the Royal Opera House, Covent Garden. Since then he has sung with many of the greatest conductors, both at Covent Garden and in the major opera houses and concert halls throughout the world.

He was the first British bass to sing the title role in Moussorgsky's *Boris Godunov* in 1983 and made history when in 1990 this production (Andrei Tarkovsky) went to the Kirov Opera in St Petersburg and was televised internationally.

He has written and presented a number of radio and TV programmes on opera and the voice.

Robert Lloyd was created a Commander of the British Empire (CBE) in 1991.

Malcolm Tibber established the National Discography and is now its Senior Repertoire Manager. He has worked for many years in the field of music recording Copyright for Polydor, Philips, RCA and WEA, for whom he was Copyright Manager.

In 1976 he founded the Philharmonia Club to support the Philharmonia Orchestra, from which developed the Friends of the Philharmonia. As the Club's Chairman he has hosted interviews with Lorin Maazel, Riccardo Muti, Simon Rattle and Paul Tortelier.

Jon Tolansky was for many years a professional musician, co-principal percussion in the Royal Opera Orchestra, and also playing in the major London orchestras. Since 1987 he has been the Administrator of the Music Performance Research Centre. He also is a frequent broadcaster and lecturer in the UK and USA.

Basil Tschaikov has had a long career as an orchestral and chamber music clarinettist. In 1943 he joined the London Philharmonic Orchestra, leaving in 1947 to join Sir Thomas Beecham's recently formed Royal Philharmonic Orchestra. From 1958 until he ceased playing in 1979 he was a member of the Philharmonia

Orchestra (Chairman 1974–79). In 1979 he was appointed Artistic and Executive Director of the National Centre for Orchestral Studies, at the University of London, Goldsmiths' College.

He was a professor of clarinet at the Royal College of Music from 1964 until 1984 and has two tutors for clarinet and many articles and chapters in books published.

Since 1987 he has been Chairman of the Music Performance Research Centre.

Musical Performance,
1996, Vol. 1, Part 1, pp. 101–106
Reprints available directly from the publisher
Photocopying permitted by license only

Index

MUSICAL PERFORMANCE
AN INTERNATIONAL JOURNAL

Notes for contributors

Submission of a paper will be taken to imply that it represents original work not previously published, that it is not being considered for publication elsewhere and that, if accepted for publication, it will not be published elsewhere in the same form, in any language, without the consent of editor and publisher. It is a condition of acceptance by the editor of a typescript for publication that the publisher automatically acquires the copyright of the typescript throughout the world. It will also be assumed that the author has obtained all necessary permissions to include in the paper items such as quotations, musical examples, figures, tables etc. Permissions should be paid for prior to submission.

Typescripts. Papers should be submitted in triplicate to the Editors, *Musical Performance, c/o* Harwood Academic Publishers, at:

5th Floor, Reading Bridge House Reading Bridge Approach Reading RG1 8PP UK	or	820 Town Center Drive Langhorne PA 19047 USA	or	3-14-9, Okubo Shinjuku-ku Tokyo 169 Japan

Papers should be typed or word processed with double spacing on one side of good quality ISO A4 (212 x 297 mm) paper with a 3 cm left-hand margin. Papers are accepted only in English.

Abstracts and Keywords. Each paper requires an abstract of 100-150 words summarizing the significant coverage and findings, presented on a separate sheet of paper. Abstracts should be followed by up to six key words or phrases which, between them, should indicate the subject matter of the paper. These will be used for indexing and data retrieval purposes.

Figures. All figures (photographs, schema, charts, diagrams and graphs) should be numbered with consecutive arabic numerals, have descriptive captions and be mentioned in the text. Figures should be kept separate from the text but an approximate position for each should be indicated in the margin of the typescript. It is the author's responsibility to obtain permission for any reproduction from other sources.

Preparation: Line drawings must be of a high enough standard for direct reproduction; photocopies are not acceptable. They should be prepared in black (india) ink on white art paper, card or tracing paper, with all the lettering and symbols included. Computer-generated graphics of a similar high quality are also acceptable, as are good sharp photoprints ("glossies"). Computer print-outs must be completely legible. Photographs intended for halftone reproduction must be good glossy original prints of maximum contrast. Redrawing or retouching of unusable figures will be charged to authors.

Size: Figures should be planned so that they reduce to 12 cm column width. The preferred width of line drawings is 24 cm, with capital lettering 4 mm high, for reduction by one-half. Photographs for halftone reproduction should be approximately twice the desired finished size.

Captions: A list of figure captions, with the relevant figure numbers, should be typed on a separate sheet of paper and included with the typescript.

Musical examples: Musical examples should be designated as "Figure 1" etc., and the recommendations above for preparation and sizing should be followed. Examples must be well prepared and of a high standard for reproduction, as they will not be redrawn or retouched by the printer.

In the case of large scores, musical examples will have to be reduced in size and so some clarity will be lost. This should be borne in mind especially with orchestral scores.

Notes are indicated by superior arabic numerals without parentheses. The text of the notes should be collected at the end of the paper.

References are indicated in the text by the name and date system either "Recent work (Smith & Jones, 1987, Robinson, 1985, 1987) . . ." or "Recently Smith & Jones (1987) . . ." If a publication has more than three authors, list all names on the first occurrence; on subsequent occurrences use the first author's name plus "*et al.*" Use an ampersand rather than "and" between the last two authors. If there is more than one publication by the same author(s) in the same year, distinguish by adding a, b, c etc. to both the text citation and the list of references (e.g. "Smith, 1986a") References should be collected and typed in alphabetical order after the Notes and Acknowledgements sections (if these exist). Examples:

Benedetti, J. (1988) *Stanislavski*, London: Methuen

Granville-Barker, H. (1934) Shakespeare's dramatic art. In *A Companion to Shakespeare Studies*, edited by H. Granville-Barker and G. B. Harrison, p. 84. Cambridge: Cambridge University Press

Johnston, D. (1970) Policy in theatre. *Hibernia*, **16**, 16

Proofs. Authors will receive page proofs (including figures) by air mail for correction and these must be returned as instructed within 48 hours of receipt. Please ensure that a full postal address is given on the first page of the typescript so that proofs are not delayed in the post. Authors' alterations, other than those of a typographical nature, in excess of 10% of the original composition cost, will be charged to authors.

Page Charges. There are no page charges to individuals or institutions.

MUSICAL PERFORMANCE

Aims and Scope

Musical Performance is international in scope, wide-ranging in content, and wholly non-commercial in approach. It deals with matters of concern to performers and their audiences. Each topic is considered seriously and in depth, in a style suitable for professional musicians, academics and music lovers.

The journal concerns all aspects of music and provides information, discussion and research from around the world. Individual issues consider concert music, opera, ballet, theatre, dance, ceremonial, jazz and popular music – folk and commercial, the interactions between performers and audiences, and their respective needs.

The journal occasionally features accompanying video or audio material.

Notes for contributors can be found at the back of the journal.

Ordering Information

Each volume is comprised of an irregular number of parts depending upon size. Issues are available individually as well as by subscription. 1996 Volume(s): 1

Orders may be placed with your usual supplier or with International Publishers Distributor at one of the addresses shown below. Journal subscriptions are sold on a per volume basis only. Claims for nonreceipt of issues will be honored free of charge if made within three months of publication of the issue. Subscriptions are available for microform editions; details will be furnished upon request.

All issues are dispatched by airmail throughout the world.

Subscription Rates

Base list subscription price per volume: ECU 65.00 (US $84.00).* This price is available only to individuals whose library subscribes to the journal OR who warrant that the journal is for their own use and provide a home address for mailing. Orders must be sent directly to the Publisher and payment must be made by personal check or credit card.

Separate rates apply to academic and corporate/government institutions, and may also include photocopy license and postage and handling charges.

*ECU (European Currency Unit) is the worldwide base list currency rate; payment can be made by draft drawn on ECU currency in the amount shown or in local currency at the current conversion rate. The US Dollar rate is based upon the ECU rate and applies to North American subscribers only. Subscribers from other territories should contact their agents or the Publisher. All prices are subject to change without notice.